Woodworking is one of the most satisfying of hobbies, and wood is the most commonly used material in home remodeling, renovating, and repair work. The best tools and techniques won't count for much unless you understand the material they are to be used on. This manual attempts to cover wood from start to finish. It explains the properties of woods and the tools and techniques necessary for a broad list of woodworking jobs, ranging from cabinetry and furniture joints to basic home improvements and repairs.

# READER'S DIGEST
# Do-it-yourself Guide

# Working with Wood

The material in this book is taken from
**Complete Do-it-yourself Manual,**
published by The Reader's Digest Association, Inc.

ISBN 0-89577-075-X
Printed in the United States of America
Second Printing, March 1980

# Workbenches

## Back-of-door tool rack

This unit can be mounted on any closet door that has at least six inches of space between door and clothes—or shelves. Make it of ½-inch pine or plywood. Actual dimensions depend on the width of your closet door. Just be sure to leave plenty of clearance for the door to open and close. This particular unit is 32 inches high x 20 inches wide. The widest bottom dimension is eight inches. The back is of ⅛-inch pegboard. Tools can be hung from hooks inserted into pegboard or holes and slots cut into the cross supports. The holes should vary in size from ½ to ¼ inch and be elongated to hold such tools as chisels and files. The drawer can be sectioned for nails, screws, and other small hardware.

Center the rack on the door; mount it slightly above the knob with four long screws. Be sure to drive them into the solid part of the door. If necessary, span the hollow part with two battens screwed into the solid part and mount the rack on these.

## Simple workbench

This six-foot-long workbench can be easily built of 2 x 4s and ¾ inch plywood. First cut the 2 x 4s for the legs, using four pieces for each, cut to the size on the drawing. Next cut the two stretchers. Secure the leg sections with dowels and glue, then fasten them to the stretchers with four 6-x-⅜-inch bolts, passing them through holes drilled in the stretchers. Cut four pipe stubs from ¾-inch pipe and install into stretchers at points indicated in drawing. Each stub has a hole drilled in it for the bolts. This avoids the need to drive screws into end grain, which has very little holding strength.

The top is made of two pieces of ¾-inch fir plywood, covered with ¼-inch-thick hardboard. Back board and shelf complete the construction.

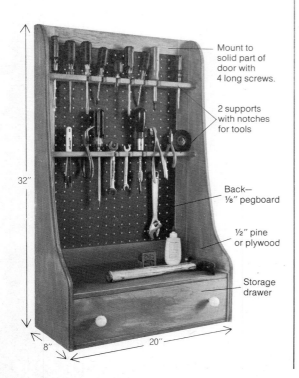

Mount to solid part of door with 4 long screws.

2 supports with notches for tools

Back— ⅛" pegboard

½" pine or plywood

Storage drawer

32"

8"    20"

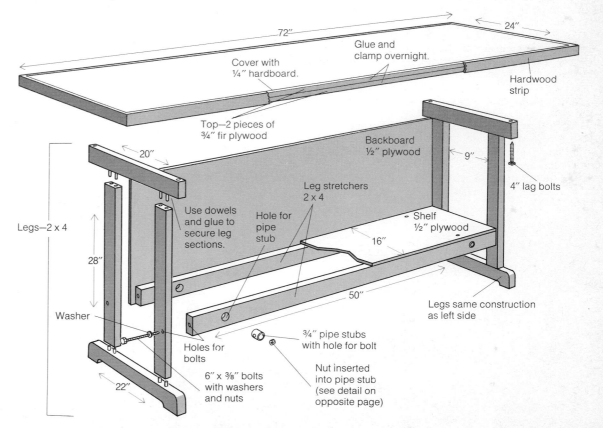

72"    24"

Glue and clamp overnight.

Cover with ¼" hardboard.

Hardwood strip

Top—2 pieces of ¾" fir plywood

Backboard ½" plywood

9"

4" lag bolts

20"

Leg stretchers 2 x 4

Legs—2 x 4

Use dowels and glue to secure leg sections.

Hole for pipe stub

Shelf ½" plywood

16"

28"

Washer

Holes for bolts

50"

Legs same construction as left side

¾" pipe stubs with hole for bolt

Nut inserted into pipe stub (see detail on opposite page)

22"

6" x ⅜" bolts with washers and nuts

## Advanced workbench

If you are a bit more ambitious, you can build this capacious workbench. Three drawers and a three-shelf cabinet give you ample storage space for tools, hardware, and paints. The first step: Making the end frames and bottom members. The end frames are attached to the bottom members with 6-inch bolts. Lag bolts, or long wood screws, could be used but this would mean forcing screws into end grain, which has little holding strength. Instead, four pipe stubs were cut from ¾-inch pipe and a hole drilled in each for a ⅜-inch bolt. The bolt passes through the leg of the end frame, into a predrilled hole in the bottom member, and through the hole in the pipe stub. A nut completes the assembly.

The top consists of two ¾-inch sheets of fir plywood topped with ¼-inch thick hardboard. Glue and clamp these together and let dry overnight. If you like, you can dress up the finished top by gluing a strip of oak or other hardwood around the sides to hide the edge grain of the plywood.

Make the drawer compartments before you make the drawers; it is easier to fit a drawer to a compartment than the other way around. Each is fitted with a center guide and slides on two plastic-laminate runners.

A back panel covers the space between the drawer section and the cabinet section. You can vary the dimensions of the cabinet areas to fit your own particular space requirements but, as a general guide, bear in mind that 36 inches is the ideal height for a workbench.

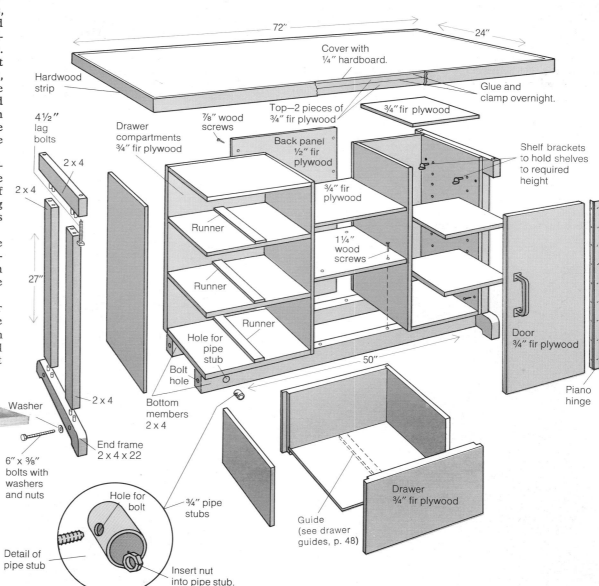

Hardwood strip

Cover with ¼" hardboard.

Glue and clamp overnight.

¾" fir plywood

4½" lag bolts

2 x 4

2 x 4

Drawer compartments ¾" fir plywood

⅞" wood screws

Top—2 pieces of ¾" fir plywood

Back panel ½" fir plywood

Shelf brackets to hold shelves to required height

¾" fir plywood

Runner

1¼" wood screws

Runner

27"

Runner

Hole for pipe stub

Bolt hole

2 x 4

50"

Door ¾" fir plywood

Piano hinge

Washer

Bottom members 2 x 4

6" x ⅜" bolts with washers and nuts

End frame 2 x 4 x 22

Hole for bolt

¾" pipe stubs

Insert nut into pipe stub.

Detail of pipe stub

Drawer ¾" fir plywood

Guide (see drawer guides, p. 48)

# Saws and sawing

## Types of saws

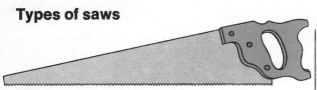

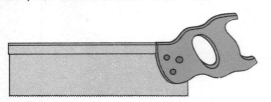

**Hand saws** for crosscutting or ripping come in two blade patterns. Upper edge of straight back pattern, above, can serve as line marker. Skew-backed type, not suited for marking, is preferred by some because saw seems more flexible.

**The backsaw,** used for joint cutting, has reinforced back edge to keep blade rigid. Typical lengths are 10 to 16 in. A longer version called a miter box saw runs from 22 to 26 in. To cut smoothly, teeth are finer than on crosscut or rip saws.

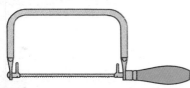

**Coping saws,** for cutting small-diameter curves, have spring steel frames with tension adjustment to hold blades taut. Blades are 1/16 to 1/8 in. wide, and from 6 to 6⅝ in. long. The blades mount to face in any direction.

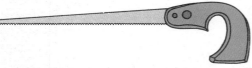

**Compass saw** has narrow, tapered blade for cutting curves or starting from bored hole. It is similar to the keyhole saw, which was once used to cut keyholes in wooden doors.

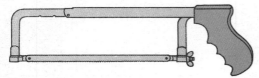

**The hacksaw,** for metal cutting, has a rigid frame that fits blades 8 to 12 in. long. High-speed steel blade mounts with teeth slanted away from handle and is drawn taut by wingnut.

## Using the crosscut saw

A crosscut saw's performance depends on the quality of the saw and how you use it. In a high-quality crosscut saw, the teeth are usually precision-ground to tiny points that cut sharply across the wood fibers. The teeth of a low-priced saw, though the same shape, are rarely precision-ground. Quality saws cut faster with the same effort from you. The number of teeth per inch, referred to as points, commonly ranges from 7 to 12. (A saw that has 7 teeth to the

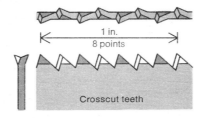

Crosscut teeth

inch is called a 7-point saw.) When a saw has a low point number, it cuts fast but leaves a rough surface. High-number saws work more slowly but are smoother-cutting. For average work, 7 or 8 points is usual; for finer work, 10 points.

To reduce sawing friction and boost efficiency, alternate teeth are set (bent) outward about ¼ the blade thickness to opposite sides. This results in a cut slightly wider than blade thickness and lets the saw cut freely.

To begin a cut, use the butt portion of the blade

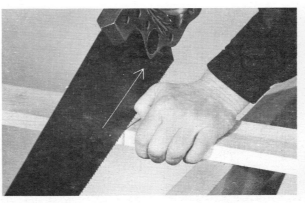

**Plywood should be cut** with a crosscut saw regardless of the direction of the surface grain. When sawing any wood, use your thumb to guide the draw strokes at the start.

near the handle. Use several pulling strokes to make a starting groove. Don't cut on the marked line, but on the waste (throwaway) side. This minimizes the chance of cutting short. Continue with full strokes

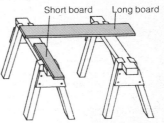

Short board    Long board

Crosscutting on sawhorses

for fast cutting and even distribution of tooth wear along the blade.

Because the crosscut saw cuts on both the forward and back strokes under its own weight, you only need to apply light pressure in using it. The most efficient cutting angle between the saw's edge and the surface of the work is 45 degrees.

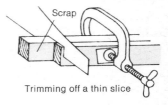

Scrap

Trimming off a thin slice

**At the finish of a crosscut,** always support the waste piece while you are making the final cut-off strokes. Never break the piece off by twisting the saw blade.

## Using a rip saw

The rip saw, designed to cut parallel to the grain, as in sawing a board lengthwise, usually has a 26-inch blade with 5½ teeth per inch. The teeth, shaped like miniature chisels with their cutting edges crosswise of the saw, literally chop their way through the wood. Alternate teeth are factory-set outward about ⅓ the blade thickness to opposite sides, to widen the cut and reduce friction.

To start a ripping cut, use the tip portion of the blade (not the butt, as with the crosscut saw), since quality rip-saw teeth are one point finer (6½) at the tip end. Use a few short pulling strokes to begin, then full strokes. Although the rip saw cuts only on the forward stroke, a sharp one can cut up to 10 feet a minute in nominal 1-inch white pine. A taper ground blade, thinner at the back edge than the toothed edge and thinner at the tip than the butt, reduces sawing effort considerably. (Available in high-quality rip and crosscut saws.) If the saw veers away from the line on long cuts, flex it slightly toward the line as you saw, to steer it back on course, but avoid sharp bending.

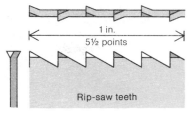

1 in.
5½ points

Rip-saw teeth

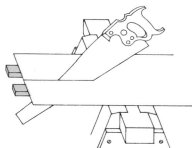

Support springy work on strips.

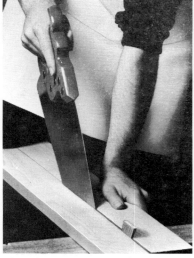

**To prevent saw jamming** in long cuts, drive wedge into starting end of cut.

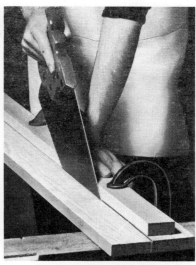

**For long ripping cuts,** saw against a batten to assure a straight cut.

## Using a backsaw

The backsaw, designed for joint-cutting work, is made in 10- to 16-inch lengths, usually with 12 or 13 teeth per inch, for smooth cuts with or across the grain. (The miter box saw is a longer version of the backsaw—up to 26 inches—and has 11 teeth per inch.)

To use a backsaw in a miter box, first mark the work for the cut, then line up the mark with the slots, to cut on the waste side of the line. Hold the work against the back of the box and start with a back stroke, holding the handle end tilted slightly upward. Level it as you proceed. To cut without a miter box, use a bench hook, as shown.

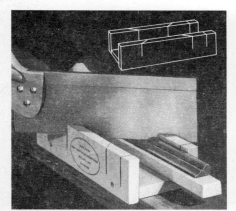

**Miter box** is used to cut moldings at 45° angles or for straight cuts. Lip seats against the front of the workbench.

**Bench hook** holds the work but doesn't guide it. Used for making straight cuts, especially when work is too large to fit miter box.

**Tenons** are rip-cut in a vise, as pictured, on the waste side of the line. Start your cut with the saw tilted over the corner.

After making the first cut, turn work around in vise to make the second cut. Saw should be straight when it reaches bottom.

# Special-purpose saws

## Coping saw—for curve cutting and filigree work

The coping saw, used for delicate ornamental and filigree work, cuts curves smaller than pencil diameter, much smaller than can be cut with a compass or keyhole saw. Its replaceable blades, usually 6 to 6⅝ inches long, depending on the saw, may be as

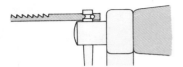

Mount blade so teeth slant to suit work

narrow as 7/100-inch, with 10 to 20 teeth per inch. (Spiral types are even slimmer.) Types are available for cutting wood, plastics, and thin metal. To change blades, turn the handle to loosen the threaded mounting grip, while springing the saw frame ends together between your body and the workbench. With frame ends sprung inward, the old blade can be removed and a new one inserted.

Slant of teeth depends on how the work is to be done. If it will be mounted vertically in a vise, the teeth should slant away from the handle, as you will be cutting on the push stroke. For exacting,

delicate scroll work, the teeth should slant toward the handle, as you will be cutting on the pull stroke. The blade can be turned during the work, without removing it from the frame, to keep the frame clear of the edge of the material as the cut changes direction. Depth between blade and back of frame is usually from 4½ to 6½ inches.

Saws with frame depths of 8 to 12 inches are sometimes called **scroll saws, fret saws,** or **deep-throat coping saws.** Their blades are mounted with teeth slanting toward the handle to cut on the pull stroke, reducing the chance of blade spring-out.

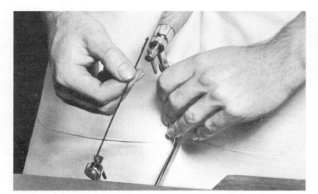

**Spring ends of coping-saw frame** towards each other to remove or replace blade. Blade holders permit turning of blade.

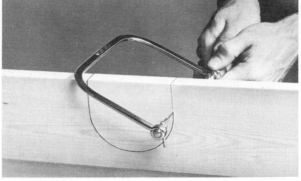

**When work is mounted vertically** in a vise for cutting, the saw teeth should be slanted away from the handle.

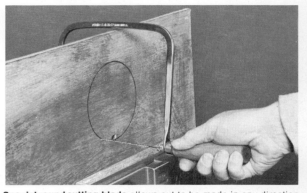

**Special round cutting blade** allows cut to be made in any direction without need for changing position of the blade.

## Compass and keyhole saws—for hole cutting

Typical compass saws have 12- to 14-inch blades with 8 or 10 teeth per inch. Keyhole saws have narrower blades, usually 10 or 12 inches long, with 10 teeth per inch. Either can cut curves, though keyhole saws cut smaller diameters than compass saws. Both are also suited to making either curved or straight cuts starting from a bored hole. Since they are not frame types, they are not limited, as a coping saw is, to working near the edge of a panel. Hence, they can be used to cut openings in floors or walls for pipes or electrical outlets with the cut starting from a bored hole. When starting from a hole, use vertical strokes to begin. As the cut progresses, bring the saw to about a 45-degree angle. When you are starting a cut from the edge, the saw can be at that approximate angle from the beginning.

**Start a cut** like this with vertical strokes in hole; tip the saw to about 45° for cut; return to vertical at corner.

## Pruning saw

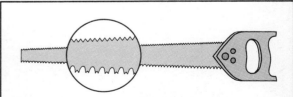

**Pruning saws** have deep-gullet teeth for cutting green wood. Straight blade types, like this, are also made with teeth on both edges—deep teeth for coarse cuts, plain 8-point crosscut teeth for trimming. Teeth slant toward tip, as on hand saws. Curved pattern pruning saws (down-curve on cutting edge) are designed for awkward places, also for use on a pole. Blade curve gives teeth back-slant for cutting on down stroke.

## Choosing and using planes

Planes are used to trim wood to size, to smooth it, to straighten irregular edges, to bevel and chamfer it, and, in special forms, to groove and shape wood into moldings. Types of planes vary according to use. The **block plane** is the smallest regular shop plane (about 6 inches long). The blade, or plane iron, is mounted bevel up at a low angle for planing along the grain or across ends. The best type for small smoothing and fitting jobs, the block plane can be operated with one hand. The **trimming plane,** usually 3½ inches long with an inch-wide blade, is for small and delicate work. A **model maker's plane,** unlike the preceding two, has a convex instead of a flat bottom, with curvatures sideways and lengthwise. It planes flat or mildly concave surfaces, is similar in size to trimming plane. The **smooth plane,** 7 to 10 inches long, has a blade about 1¾ inches wide, mounted bevel down. A cap on top of the blade bends and breaks shavings, minimizes surface roughening. Good for light to moderate general use. The **scrub plane** is sized comparably to the smooth plane but has a narrower blade (1¼ inches) with a rounded cutting edge. Choose it for fast rough cutting, also to produce a hand-hewn effect. The **jack plane** averages 12 to 15 inches in length, around 2 inches in blade width. A general-use plane much like the smooth plane, it is better for edge-straightening because of its greater length. **Fore** and **jointer planes,** like the jack plane but longer (from 18 to 24 inches), are the best choice for edge straightening.

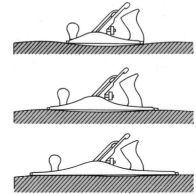

**Small plane,** such as block plane, rides up and down waves of irregular edge.

**Longer jack plane** spans several crests, has some straightening effect.

**Very long jointer plane** spans waves, cuts down high spots and straightens entire edge of work.

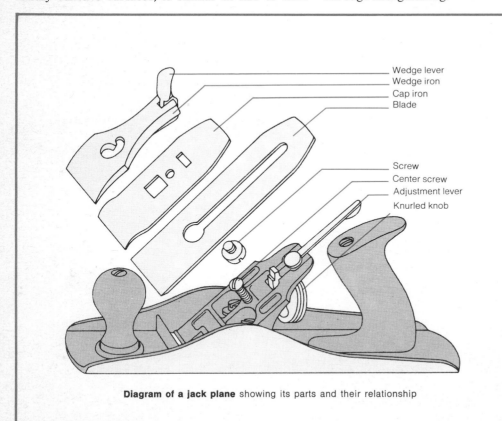

Wedge lever
Wedge iron
Cap iron
Blade

Screw
Center screw
Adjustment lever
Knurled knob

**Diagram of a jack plane** showing its parts and their relationship

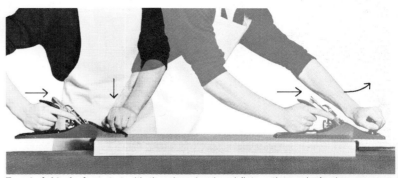

**For straight planing,** start with the plane level and flat on the work. Apply even pressure during the stroke to produce a continuous shaving. Hold the plane nose up at the end of the stroke to prevent a down curve. Always plane in direction of grain to minimize chipping. Planing against grain leaves rough surface.

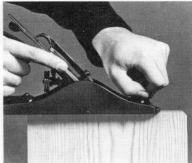

**To chamfer or bevel** using a plane, first mark the work, then tip the plane as shown. Plane with the grain.

**On end grain,** plane from the edges toward the center. Then plane off the hump in the center to level edge.

# Planes

## Block planes

Although the basic block plane types are described as adjustable and nonadjustable, both of them can be adjusted. Cut depth is increased or decreased on the adjustable type by turning the adjusting wheel to loosen the blade, moving it in or out by hand and re-tightening the wheel. On either type, alignment of blade cutting edge with plane mouth must be done by hand with the blade loose. Block planes of the nonadjustable type are lower-priced, but the adjustable type is more convenient.

To plane across the end grain of a board, set the plane iron for a shallow cut, making sure the iron is sharp. Before starting the cut, be sure to bevel the ends slightly. This is important. If you don't, the plane will split the wood as it nears the end of the cut. Make the bevel cut with the plane at a 45-degree angle.

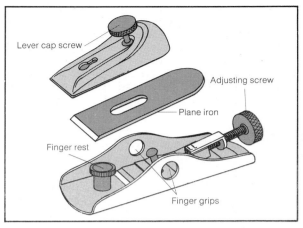

Lever cap screw

Adjusting screw

Plane iron

Finger rest

Finger grips

**On end grain** and wavy grain, hold block plane at 15° angle to direction of motion to cut with a minimum of wood roughening

## Blade adjustment

To remove a lot of material, set for deep cut at the start, shallow at the finish. If the grain isn't apparent, check the surface after the first stroke. If it is roughened noticeably, plane the opposite way. On wavy grain, set for a shallow cut, and plane at an angle. For general work, set the plane iron cap (on large planes) about $\frac{1}{16}$ inch back from cutting edge; on curly wood, as close to edge as possible but not on it. To sharpen a large plane iron, grind only the original bevel, leaving top flat.

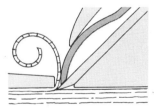

Plane iron cap breaks and curls shavings.

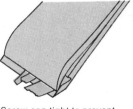

Screw cap tight to prevent wedged shavings.

**To align blade** for even-width cut, sight along bottom and set cutting edge parallel to plane mouth. Move blade by hand on block plane, by lateral adjusting lever on larger plane types.

## Using a shooting board

**Shooting board** is made by nailing one square-edged board higher than another on crosspieces, as shown in the drawing below, with a stop block at one end. With the work resting on the upper board, and end edge projecting, a plane can be tipped on its side and slid along the lower board to trim the work edge perfectly square.

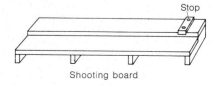

Stop

Shooting board

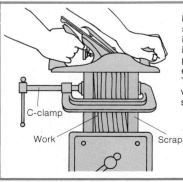

C-clamp

Work

Scrap

**Easy way** to prevent splitting of corners in end-grain planing is with scrap pieces clamped on each side of the work. The scrap, not the work, does the splitting.

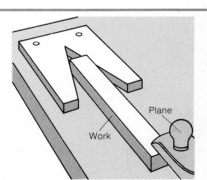

Plane

Work

**Jig to hold work** for planing consists of piece of wood with a V cut out and screwed to bench top. Jig accepts work equal to width slightly less than V opening.

## How to use a rabbet plane

The rabbet plane makes a cut as wide as its bottom, descending into the cut as it deepens. Guided by a fence, or a batten on the work, it can cut a recessed step in the surface of a board adjoining the edge. Each stroke deepens the recess until the required depth is reached. For across-the-grain planing, a sharp spur attachment is used to score the edge of the cut and prevent tearing of fibers.

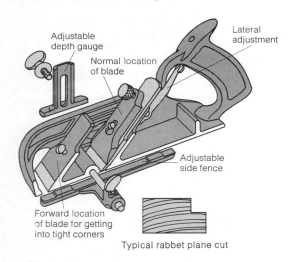

Adjustable depth gauge

Lateral adjustment

Normal location of blade

Adjustable side fence

Forward location of blade for getting into tight corners

Typical rabbet plane cut

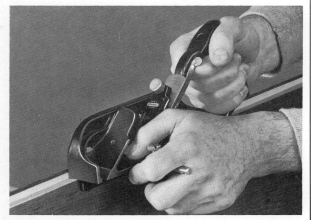

**Rabbet plane is used** to cut a recessed groove along the surface of a board along the edge. Cutter can be set to make a groove in a board even though board butts up against a wall.

## How to use a hand router

The hand router is used chiefly to even and smooth the bottom of a squared groove, such as might receive the end of a shelf, after the material has been roughed out between saw cuts, usually with a chisel. The **open-throat router plane** shown below has an adjustable guide fence. The smaller **hand router** can be guided by a batten on the work. Cutting depth can be increased in steps to final level.

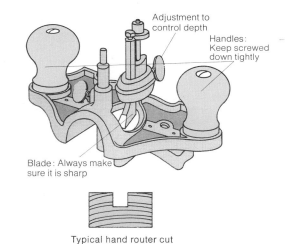

Adjustment to control depth

Handles: Keep screwed down tightly

Blade: Always make sure it is sharp

Typical hand router cut

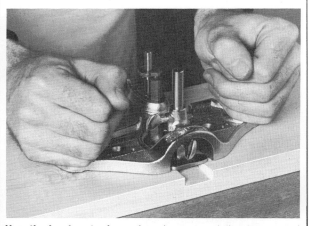

**How the hand router is used** to clean out a dado after most of the stock has been removed with a number of saw cuts. Cutting action consists of a series of short forward strokes.

## How to use a spokeshave

The spokeshave is used to smooth or chamfer curved edges, convex or concave. Blade cutting depth is set by hand on some models, by screw adjustment on others. To use: With work in a vise, grasp both handles and push or pull along work. As a spokeshave must cut with the grain, it is often pushed along one section, then pulled along the other, to the center, to avoid having to shift work in the vise. Since the spokeshave is a kind of plane, the cutter must be kept sharp to do its job. Sharpen it as you would sharpen a plane iron (p. 10). Oil on the cutting edge, when tool is not in use, will prevent rusting.

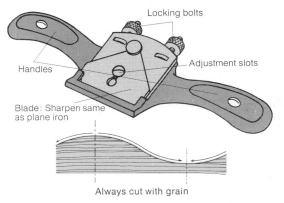

Locking bolts

Handles

Adjustment slots

Blade: Sharpen same as plane iron

Always cut with grain

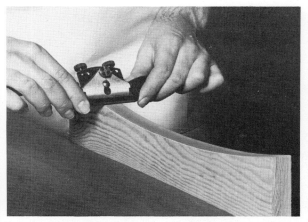

**To use a spokeshave** for cutting a concave curve, work from each end of the board toward the center. Always cut with grain and have blade at slight angle. Be sure blade is sharp.

# Special-purpose planes

## Surform tools and their uses

Surform tools can be used plane- or file-fashion on wood, aluminum, copper, brass, plastic, laminates, and similar materials. (Shavings pass through the blade into the recess above, so the tool is used as a cheese grater by some.) Because of multiple cutting edges, the replaceable blades are well suited to end-grain cutting and smoothing of convex surfaces. Use with light to moderate pressure.

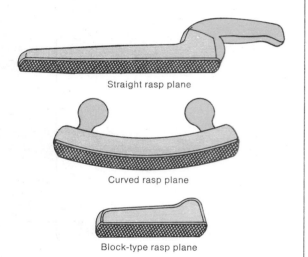

Straight rasp plane

Curved rasp plane

Block-type rasp plane

**Surform, or rasp planes** come in several styles and lengths. Handled in use like an ordinary plane; cannot, however, be adjusted for depth of cut. Less expensive than planes.

## Using a drawknife

The drawknife removes material rapidly, operating somewhat like a spokeshave but taking much heavier cuts. It is held by the handles and drawn toward the user, with cutting depth controlled by the angle of the handles. It can be used to rough-cut large pieces prior to planing, as in removing large corner portions from square lumber at the start of rounding. Cutting edge widths run 10 to 12 inches.

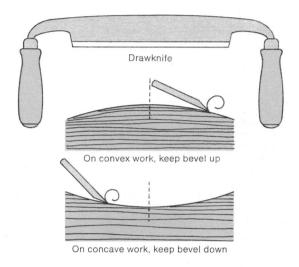

Drawknife

On convex work, keep bevel up

On concave work, keep bevel down

**How the drawknife is used.** Work should be securely held in a vise. Chief advantage of the drawknife is that it can cut right up to any obstruction on the work.

## How to sharpen and hone a plane

Chisels and plane irons have two angles forming their cutting edge, a 25-degree ground angle and a 30-degree honed angle. Ground angle is formed on a grindstone and only needs occasional renewing. Honed angle is formed and maintained by rubbing on an oilstone. To hone a chisel or plane iron, oil the stone, then hold the blade at about a 30-degree angle to the stone, rubbing it to and fro along its length.

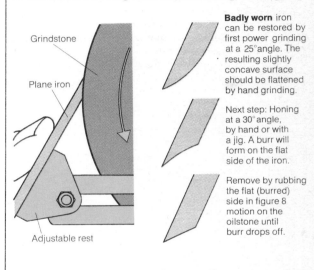

Grindstone

Plane iron

Adjustable rest

**Badly worn** iron can be restored by first power grinding at a 25°angle. The resulting slightly concave surface should be flattened by hand grinding.

Next step: Honing at a 30°angle, by hand or with a jig. A burr will form on the flat side of the iron.

Remove by rubbing the flat (burred) side in figure 8 motion on the oilstone until burr drops off.

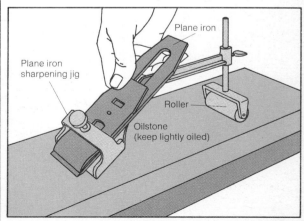

Plane iron

Plane iron sharpening jig

Roller

Oilstone (keep lightly oiled)

**Jig for honing a plane iron** keeps the iron at predetermined angle to the stone, generally 30°. The stone should be kept lubricated with light machine oil during honing process.

## Types of chisels

Most chisels today have plastic handles which can be struck with a hammer or with a mallet without danger of splitting. In fact, some chisels for use on wood are made of one-piece steel. Size is a factor in selection. The shortest is the **butt chisel,** about 7 to 9 inches long, for use in tight spaces. Next is the 9-to-10½-inch **pocket chisel,** preferred for general shop work. Largest is the **mill chisel,** 16 inches long, good for heavy work but seldom used in the home shop. Intended purpose is the other basic consideration. The **paring chisel** is thin-bladed, new-ground to a 25-degree edge, often re-ground to 15 degrees. Drive it by hand only for precise shave cuts in fitting work. The **firmer chisel** has a thick blade for heavy driving. The **gouge** is a hollow-blade type. **Firmer gouges** may be bevel-ground inside or outside, **paring gouges** are bevel-ground inside only.

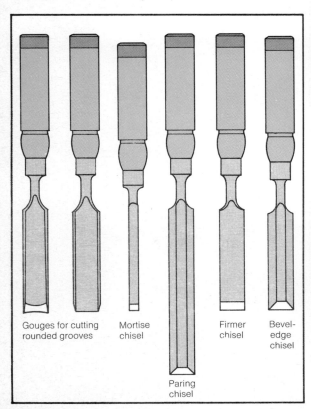

Gouges for cutting rounded grooves

Mortise chisel

Paring chisel

Firmer chisel

Bevel-edge chisel

## Using chisels

Work only with sharp chisels, and use them only for material removal that other tools cannot do. In lap-joint work, make close parallel saw cuts across the joint area, not quite to joint depth, and remove the material between the saw cuts. Then pare down to joint level with a chisel. In cutting a mortise, first score the outline with a knife so any surface splitting won't extend beyond it. Then bore out the bulk of the wood within the outline with an auger bit. Use the chisel to remove the rest and to finish the mortise to size and shape. Shallow recesses, such as for lock strike plates, can be made with a chisel by a series of close cross-grain cuts (within a knife outline), followed by paring cuts.

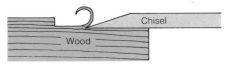

If the area to be cut extends to the end of the work chisel with bevel facing out, toward the waste

If the area is enclosed, it may be necessary to use the chisel with the bevel facing inward

**Using a chisel** and a mallet to cut a mortise. First step is to drill a series of holes slightly narrower than required width. Then use chisel to clear out waste.

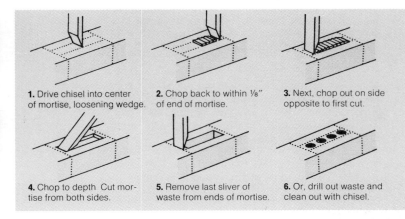

**1.** Drive chisel into center of mortise, loosening wedge.

**2.** Chop back to within ⅛" of end of mortise.

**3.** Next, chop out on side opposite to first cut.

**4.** Chop to depth Cut mortise from both sides.

**5.** Remove last sliver of waste from ends of mortise.

**6.** Or, drill out waste and clean out with chisel.

**Hold a chisel** so that the beveled edge faces the waste part of the wood. Start in at the extreme waste side of the wood and gradually work toward marking line.

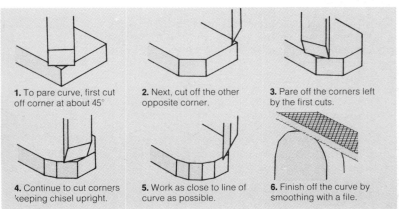

**1.** To pare curve, first cut off corner at about 45°

**2.** Next, cut off the other opposite corner.

**3.** Pare off the corners left by the first cuts.

**4.** Continue to cut corners keeping chisel upright.

**5.** Work as close to line of curve as possible.

**6.** Finish off the curve by smoothing with a file.

# Vises and clamps

## Types of bench vises

Bench vises are made in both **bolt-on** and **clamp-on** models. Bases may be either **rigid** or **swivel** types. For light duty, especially where a permanently installed vise might be an obstacle, it is best to select a clamp-on vise. For full-range use, buy a bolt-mounted vise, preferably one that has regular and pipe jaws, and a jaw width and opening of at least 3½ inches. Specialized vises include **vacuum-base** types that lock to any smooth surface and **multi-angle** vises which swivel horizontally and can be tilted vertically to any required position.

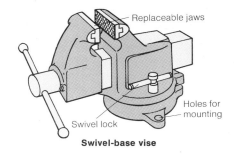

Replaceable jaws
Swivel lock
Holes for mounting

**Swivel-base vise**

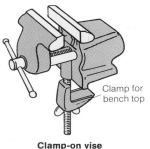

Clamp for bench top

**Clamp-on vise**

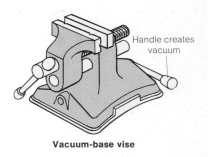

Handle creates vacuum

**Vacuum-base vise**

## Woodworking vises

Woodworkers' vises do not mount on top of the workbench, as bench vises do, but at the edge of the bench, with their jaw tops flush with the bench top. Mounted in this way, they do not obstruct large work on the bench.

Jaws of woodworkers' vises are lined with wood or hardboard to protect the work clamped between them. A useful feature on some: A half thread that makes it possible to slide the jaw against the work without a lot of handle turning. The vise is then tightened with only a half turn.

When mounting a woodworking vise to a workbench, use heavy lag screws, which can be tightened with a wrench, instead of ordinary wood screws.

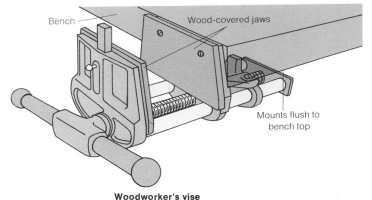

Bench
Wood-covered jaws
Mounts flush to bench top

**Woodworker's vise**

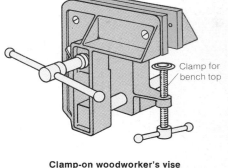

Clamp for bench top

**Clamp-on woodworker's vise**

## The versatile C-clamp

As a rule, C-clamps are made in sizes from 1 to 8 inches. (Sizes are based on the maximum opening.) The depth to the back of the clamp usually ranges from 1 inch to about 4 inches, depending on the size of the clamp. Deep-throated types are available, however, from some manufacturers.

Always insert pads of scrap wood between the clamp jaws and the work to protect the work's surface against marring. These protective pads also serve to distribute pressure uniformly. The ball joint at the foot of the clamp is designed to swivel so that work which is not absolutely flat can still be securely clamped. Buy C-clamps as required in sizes to suit each job as it comes up. After a few projects, you will have all the sizes you need.

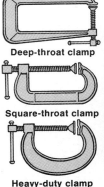

**Deep-throat clamp**

**Square-throat clamp**

**Heavy-duty clamp**

**Wood** between work and clamp jaws protects finish.

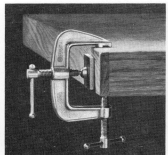

**This clamp** applies pressure in two directions for edge gluing.

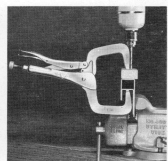

**Vise-grip clamp,** handy for holding any irregularly-shaped work.

## Adjustable hand screws

Termed hand screws, these woodworking clamps have maple jaws that do not require pads of scrap wood to protect the work. Since the steel clamping screws operate through crosswise pivots in the wood jaws, they can be set at any required angle. Sizes, based on jaw length, range from 6 to 14 inches, openings from 3 to 10 inches, though the full size range is not stocked by all suppliers.

To open or close the hand screws, place the jaws' square ends toward you and grasp the right-hand spindle handle in your right hand, the left in your left hand. Rotate the entire clamp, "cranking" with your right hand, in the required direction to open or close the jaws evenly to the approximate gap. Then make final tightening adjustments.

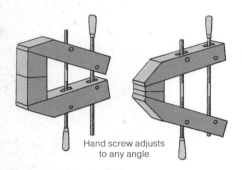

Hand screw adjusts to any angle

If new clamps have oil-finished jaws, clamp them tightly against blotting or other absorbent paper on a block before using them on actual work.

**An adjustable hand screw** is used to apply pressure to drawer guides while glue sets overnight. Avoid excessive pressure.

## Spring clamps

Small spring clamps are the simplest type of gripping device to use on light-duty work where high clamping pressure is not required, as with modern gap-filler glues. The overall length of these clamps usually ranges from a little over 4 inches to about 8¼ inches, jaw openings from ⅞ inch to 3 inches. They are perfectly suited to fast-setting glue jobs where many clamps must be applied quickly. Some spring clamps have vinyl-covered jaws to protect the work from marring. Don't underrate the strength of these clamps. Some large ones have very heavy springs and actually require two hands to open.

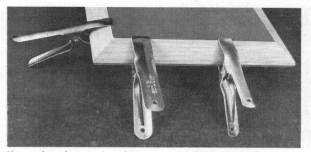

**Use spring clamps** where heavy pressure is not required.

## Bar and pipe-bar clamps

Bar-type clamps (also called **cabinet** or **furniture clamps**) are made two ways: With jaws mounted on a flat steel bar, in 12- to 48-inch lengths; and with jaws designed to fit ½- and ¾-inch steel pipe. In the latter, the clamp assembly can be made to size by cutting pipe to length and threading one end. One jaw in both types has a clamping screw. To use the clamp, set the fixed jaw against one side of the work and slide the movable jaw against the other side, then tighten clamp with the hand screw.

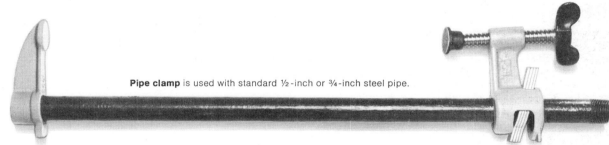

**Pipe clamp** is used with standard ½-inch or ¾-inch steel pipe.

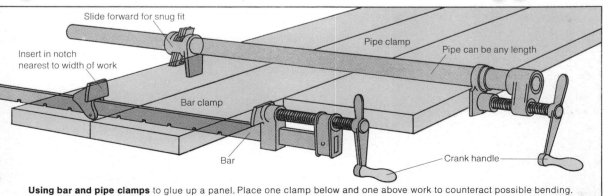

Slide forward for snug fit

Insert in notch nearest to width of work

Pipe clamp

Pipe can be any length

Bar clamp

Bar

Crank handle

**Using bar and pipe clamps** to glue up a panel. Place one clamp below and one above work to counteract possible bending.

# Vises and clamps

## Band and web clamps

Clamps designed to tighten a fabric band (canvas or nylon) around the work are used to clamp irregular shapes and, simultaneously, to draw together several joints, as in gluing chair rungs. Band length commonly ranges from 12 to 15 feet. In clamping, the band is placed around the work and pulled snug at the clamp body, then tightened by a crank or ratchet mechanism, depending on the type and make.

**Band clamp** holds the chair parts in the correct position while the glue sets.

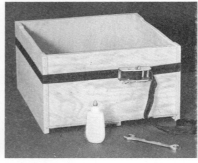

**Assembling and gluing** of a drawer is simplified by use of the band clamp.

**Nylon band clamp** is tightened by means of a wrench, which is applied as shown.

## Homemade clamping devices

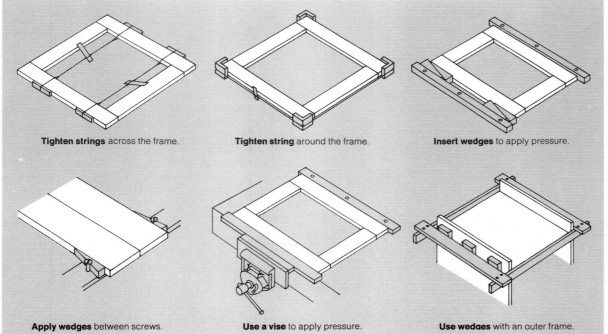

**Tighten strings** across the frame.

**Tighten string** around the frame.

**Insert wedges** to apply pressure.

**Apply wedges** between screws.

**Use a vise** to apply pressure.

**Use wedges** with an outer frame.

## Special clamps

The **hold-down** is attached to a countersunk bolt on the workbench. When not needed, it is removed from the bolt, leaving the bench top clear. **Edge clamps** are useful where the work is too wide or long to use a C clamp or pipe clamp. After the bar clamp is attached, the edge clamp, shaped to fit it, is inserted. **Miter clamps** hold mitered joints while glue sets.

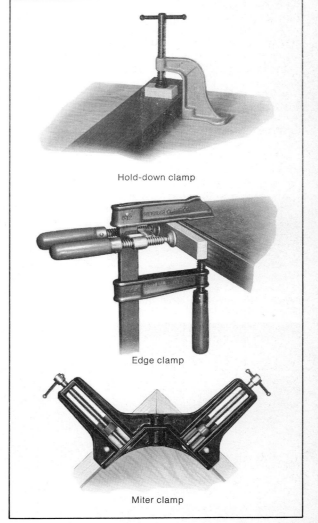

Hold-down clamp

Edge clamp

Miter clamp

## Coated abrasives

Modern coated abrasives include silicon carbide (hardest and sharpest, but brittle), aluminum oxide, garnet, flint, and emery. Abrasives come backed with cloth (stronger and more flexible) or paper, in standard and "wet" types (residue washes away). The abrasive particles may be close together (closed coat) for average work, or spaced widely apart (open coat) for materials that tend to clog. To hand sand heavily painted or pitchy surfaces, use inexpensive flint paper, discarding it as it clogs; hand sand clean wood with garnet paper, which is also low-priced. For power sanding of wood, aluminum oxide is fast and long-lasting. Silicon carbide cuts soft metals and plastics with light pressure, also rounds off the sharp edges of glass. For metal polishing, emery is customary. The work determines abrasiveness—very coarse for fast stock removal, fine for finishing.

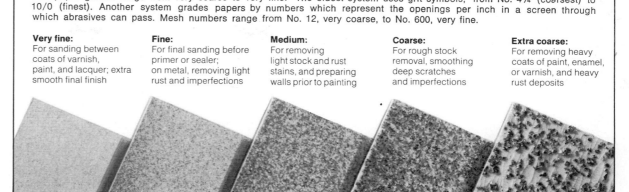

Sandpaper grades range from very coarse to very fine. The oldest system uses grit symbols, from No. 4¼ (coarsest) to 10/0 (finest). Another system grades papers by numbers which represent the openings per inch in a screen through which abrasives can pass. Mesh numbers range from No. 12, very coarse, to No. 600, very fine.

**Very fine:**
For sanding between coats of varnish, paint, and lacquer; extra smooth final finish

**Fine:**
For final sanding before primer or sealer; on metal, removing light rust and imperfections

**Medium:**
For removing light stock and rust stains, and preparing walls prior to painting

**Coarse:**
For rough stock removal, smoothing deep scratches and imperfections

**Extra coarse:**
For removing heavy coats of paint, enamel, or varnish, and heavy rust deposits

**Rubber sanding block** grips the paper at both ends with recessed nails, thus relieving finger pressure. Useful for rounding ends, as pad is slightly resilient.

**On wooden block,** use enough sandpaper so that fingers can grip it securely. Tear the paper against a sharp edge rather than cutting it with scissors.

**Wet-or-dry silicon-carbide** paper has waterproof backing. Used wet, it cleans and smooths metal on car bodies prior to spraying; use it dry on wood.

**A sanding shortcut** for rungs and chair legs: Fold or tear the sandpaper into long strips. With one end in each hand, use as you would a shoe polishing rag.

**Sanding pad** made of nylon fibers is mildly abrasive; useful for sanding prior to final finishing or between coats. Pads are available palm-size.

**When sanding an end,** protect other areas of wood by fastening a strip of wood at top and bottom of work. Hold strips firmly in position with C-clamps.

## Choosing the right sandpaper

**For wood, plastics, and fiber glass:**
Use aluminum oxide paper. This man-made abrasive is tough and durable and well-suited for grinding and finishing extremely hard materials. It is capable of penetrating practically any surface, is a fast-cutting paper, and will continue to cut for an exceptionally long time.

Silicon carbide, an abrasive that is even harder than aluminum oxide, is also good for sanding hard plastics, glass, and ceramics.

**For the sanding of metals:**
Use an abrasive made of silicon carbide or aluminum oxide. Both of these are man-made materials and extremely hard.

Emery sandpaper was at one time generally regarded as the best abrasive to use on metal. However, because of its slow cutting action and tendency to wear out quickly, emery has been superseded by these powerful abrasives.

Aluminum oxide is used extensively for polishing stainless steel and for finishing high-carbon steel and bronze.

Silicon carbide is the sharpest and hardest substance known. It performs excellently for grinding and finishing brass, copper, and aluminum. Silicon carbide paper can be used wet or dry. When dry, it is used like garnet or flint paper; when wet, it is long-lasting and suitable for rubbing down paint work on metal, especially auto bodies.

# Electric drills

## Choosing a drill

Because of its versatility, the electric drill is a wise choice for the homeowner's first portable power tool. It can drill metal, wood, plastic, and concrete, and perform many other operations as well.

The size of the drill is determined by the largest drill shank its chuck will accept, which may be ¼, ⅜, ½, or ¾ inch. The ¼-inch size is handiest for the average home workshop. A drill's power varies with size and make but typically ranges from about ⅓ hp in the ¼-inch size to as much as 1½ hp in ¾-inch models. Speed usually decreases with size (though turning power increases), ranging from about 2000 rpm for ¼-inch size to around 1200 rpm for ⅜ inch and 600 rpm for ½-inch drills. The ¾-inch size (largely for professional and industrial use) is commonly in the 250–475 rpm range. The slower speeds of the larger drills provide greater turning power (torque) necessary for driving large diameter bits and hole saws.

The high speed of the ¼-inch drills equips them not only to drill holes up to ¼-inch diameter in metal and ½ inch in wood, but also for sanding. Variable speed control is also available on many ¼- to ½-inch models; some ⅜- and ½-inch drills are also reversible. The speed control lets you select the best drilling speed. Reverse is useful in backing out wood bits from deep holes.

Heavy-duty drills of any given size vary more widely in price than do the light-duty models because of differences in bearings, wiring, and other features. For normal home use, heavy-duty features are not usually necessary.

Most drills are equipped with 3-wire grounding cords (with 3-prong plugs) to protect the user from shock in case of internal electrical damage. If you buy a drill with a 2-prong plug, be sure the tool is a type in which the outer shell and chuck are completely insulated from the wiring. Such drills are commonly termed double-insulated drills.

Many drills come with a polyethylene plastic carrying case which generally also contains an assortment of accessories. Whatever drill you buy, check the guarantee as well as the availability of parts. Your best guide to quality is a reputable manufacturer.

## Bits

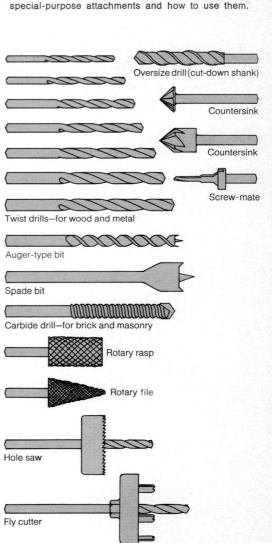

Shown below is a selection of the bits most often used in the average home workshop. Twist drills are among the most popular because they bore through both wood and metal. See the following pages for special-purpose attachments and how to use them.

Oversize drill (cut-down shank)

Countersink

Countersink

Screw-mate

Twist drills—for wood and metal

Auger-type bit

Spade bit

Carbide drill—for brick and masonry

Rotary rasp

Rotary file

Hole saw

Fly cutter

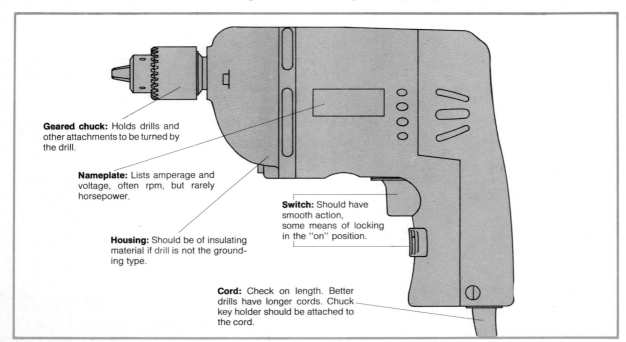

**Geared chuck:** Holds drills and other attachments to be turned by the drill.

**Nameplate:** Lists amperage and voltage, often rpm, but rarely horsepower.

**Housing:** Should be of insulating material if drill is not the grounding type.

**Switch:** Should have smooth action, some means of locking in the "on" position.

**Cord:** Check on length. Better drills have longer cords. Chuck key holder should be attached to the cord.

## How to select a circular saw

Any portable circular saw you buy for your shop should be capable of cutting a 2 x 4 at a 45-degree angle. In general, saws that have a blade diameter of 7 inches or more are good choices.

A number of other considerations have a bearing on your decision. The saw should have a depth adjustment, which enables you to make shallow cuts when required; an angle adjustment for cutting miters and bevels; and a ripping fence, which guides the saw when you want to rip a board to a specific width. It should also have an automatic spring-actuated blade guard that retracts as the blade enters the work, then covers the exposed part of the blade as soon as the cut has been completed.

Since most present-day saws have all of these features, your final choice often depends on how conveniently a saw operates and how easily the adjustments are made. Large-sized adjusting wing nuts are worthwhile details, as is an easy-to-grip handle on the blade guard. In addition to the saw handle, which contains the trigger starting switch, a knob on the end of the motor housing is convenient as an extra handle for awkward situations. This feature is not essential, however, with smaller saws.

## Safety practices

When using a portable circular saw, always be sure that the work to be cut is firmly supported, or held, so that it will not shift during the cut. Start the saw before the blade enters the work and guide it straight along the cutting line. Veering can cause jamming, stalling, even possible motor damage. (Be especially careful not to let the saw veer when you are using a masonry-cutting blade. In this case blade breakage could result.) If a long piece of wood is to be cut off, it should be supported by a helper. It must not be moved during the cut in such a way as to close the cut and bind the blade.

Keep a firm grip on the saw with your right hand, and keep your left hand well away from the saw. Make certain also that the cord is well out of the way so it will not be cut by the blade.

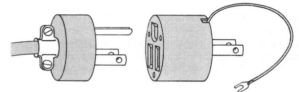

Always connect cord of three-pronged plug to properly grounded outlet or use adapter with ground wire.

Lower blade guard covers the lower part of the blade; retracts as the blade enters the work.

Maintain a strong grip on the saw to keep it from tipping or dropping at the end of the cut. Keep your hands clear of the blade during the time required for it to come to a complete stop. Never adjust the saw without first disconnecting the power cord.

When replacing a blade, make sure that it will be turning in the right direction. This is generally indicated by an arrow on the blade. Also always be sure to use a sharp blade. A dull blade requires more power to cut through the work, tends to scorch the wood, and is a hazard to use because you tend to push the saw into the wood, instead of letting the saw do the work.

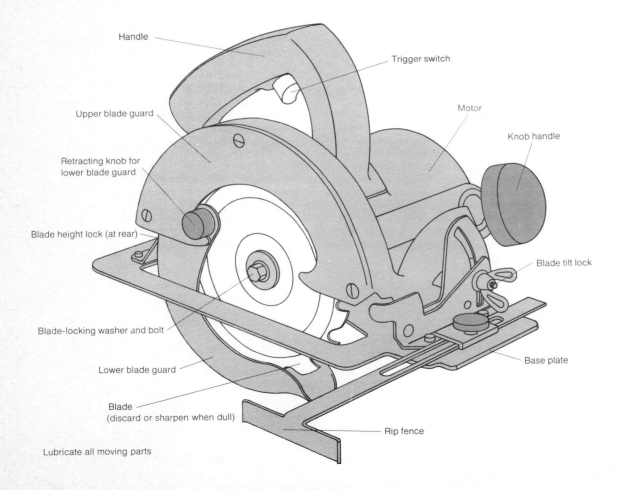

Handle

Trigger switch

Motor

Upper blade guard

Knob handle

Retracting knob for lower blade guard

Blade height lock (at rear)

Blade tilt lock

Blade-locking washer and bolt

Lower blade guard

Base plate

Blade (discard or sharpen when dull)

Rip fence

Lubricate all moving parts

# Circular power saws

## Adjusting and setting the saw

Although circular saws operate at maximum efficiency when they are adjusted to cut just through the bottom of the work, many users leave the blade at the full-depth adjustment for general work. The difference in performance is only noticeable when you are cutting thick stock.

If the tilt angle of the saw has been changed at a previous stage of the job, be sure that it is correctly readjusted. You can check for right-angle cuts by cutting a scrap piece and using a try square on the cut section. If you adjust the saw for a miter or bevel cut, test the angle by cutting a scrap piece before cutting the pieces to be actually used. A test is also advisable with shallow-depth adjustments and rip fence settings.

When trying out a new saw, familiarize yourself with all the adjustments by making several cuts on scrap wood. In this way you will learn how accurate the settings on the saw really are. The calibration on the saw, showing angles and distance, should only be used as a guide, never for actual measurements. Remember, too, that the width of the saw kerf (cut) and the types of blades used in construction work affect the precision of the final result. Use turps to remove gum, dirt, and pitch from the bottom of the saw. An occasional waxing of the bottom is a good idea. It will help the saw glide smoothly along the work. Also, make certain that the trigger switch is operating smoothly and that it does not lock inadvertently in the "on" position.

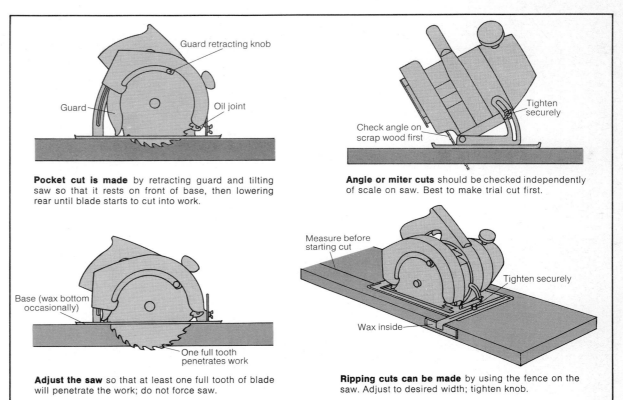

**Pocket cut is made** by retracting guard and tilting saw so that it rests on front of base, then lowering rear until blade starts to cut into work.

**Angle or miter cuts** should be checked independently of scale on saw. Best to make trial cut first.

**Adjust the saw** so that at least one full tooth of blade will penetrate the work; do not force saw.

**Ripping cuts can be made** by using the fence on the saw. Adjust to desired width; tighten knob.

## How to choose blades

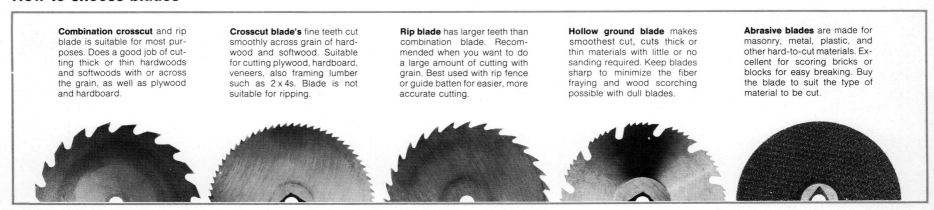

**Combination crosscut** and rip blade is suitable for most purposes. Does a good job of cutting thick or thin hardwoods and softwoods with or across the grain, as well as plywood and hardboard.

**Crosscut blade's** fine teeth cut smoothly across grain of hardwood and softwood. Suitable for cutting plywood, hardboard, veneers, also framing lumber such as 2 x 4s. Blade is not suitable for ripping.

**Rip blade** has larger teeth than combination blade. Recommended when you want to do a large amount of cutting with grain. Best used with rip fence or guide batten for easier, more accurate cutting.

**Hollow ground blade** makes smoothest cut, cuts thick or thin materials with little or no sanding required. Keep blades sharp to minimize the fiber fraying and wood scorching possible with dull blades.

**Abrasive blades** are made for masonry, metal, plastic, and other hard-to-cut materials. Excellent for scoring bricks or blocks for easy breaking. Buy the blade to suit the type of material to be cut.

## Various uses

**Crosscutting** a 2 x 4 is a common operation for the portable saw. Support the work with your left hand as you guide saw with right.

**A rip cut** is a cut made with the grain of the wood. If the cut is not too wide, you can use the rip fence as a cutting guide.

**A wide or long cut** is best made with a batten clamped to the work as shown. Press against side of batten as you move saw forward.

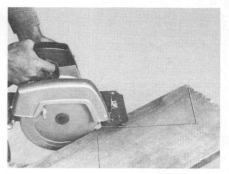

**Stringer cut for stairs** should stop before the end of the line, be finished with a handsaw. Cutting beyond mark weakens wood.

**To make a dado cut,** first mark the area to be cut away on the board, allow for blade thickness and set blade for desired depth.

After making the first cut, make the second cut at the required width. Measure carefully and use a clamped batten as a guide.

Next, make a series of parallel passes between the two outside cuts. Reset the batten (or the rip fence) as required.

To remove the waste, you can use the saw or, if you prefer, a chisel and mallet. Cuts can be made with or across the grain.

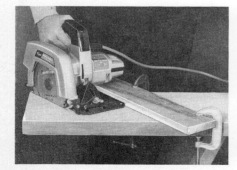

**Miter:** Clamp a straightedge over the wood to act as a miter guide fence. Make sure that the clamps will not foul the saw.

**Bevel:** Loosen the wing nut and set the saw at the desired angle, tighten the nut. Check on scrap wood before making a finish cut.

**Compound bevel:** This is a combination miter cut and a bevel cut, made at the same time. Always make trial cut first on scrap wood.

**Grooving:** Decorative cuts can be made on paneling by setting blade to make a shallow (⅛ in.-deep) cut. Use guide as shown.

# Saber saw

## Various uses

With various blades, the portable jigsaw, sometimes called a saber saw, can make straight or curved cuts in wood plywood, hardboard, laminates, light metal, and even ceramics. It will rip a long piece of wood, crosscut, bevel, miter, and start a cut in the middle of a panel. With a special blade, it will cut flush to a perpendicular surface, permitting openings near a wall for heating ducts or plumbing. Most jigsaws cut through 2-inch stock.

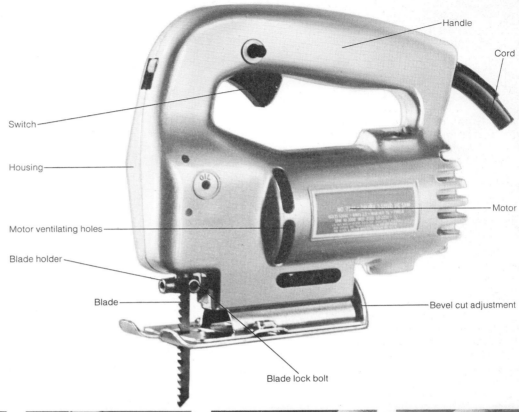

Handle
Cord
Switch
Housing
Motor
Motor ventilating holes
Blade holder
Blade
Bevel cut adjustment
Blade lock bolt

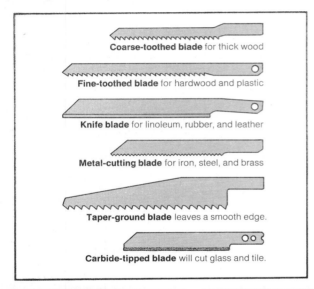

**Coarse-toothed blade** for thick wood

**Fine-toothed blade** for hardwood and plastic

**Knife blade** for linoleum, rubber, and leather

**Metal-cutting blade** for iron, steel, and brass

**Taper-ground blade** leaves a smooth edge.

**Carbide-tipped blade** will cut glass and tile.

**Pocket cut:** Tilt the saw so that the base rests firmly on the work. Then tilt the base back slowly until the blade enters the wood.

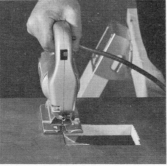

Near the end of the cut, turn the saw to make the next straight line cut and then finish off the leftover pieces in the corners.

**Bevel cut:** Loosen the adjustment at the base plate and tilt the plate to the desired angle. Tighten and use the saw in the conventional way.

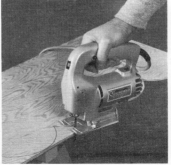

**Curved cuts:** Use narrowest blade to get sharpest curve. Start from edge, or make a pocket cut. Clamp work to prevent chattering.

**Rip cut:** Long straight cuts are termed ripping. This can be done with an accessory rip fence or with a board clamped to the work.

## How to choose and use a router

The router is basically a simple portable tool, consisting of a high-speed electric motor (about 24,000 rpm) mounted vertically on a horizontal base plate. A chuck on the lower edge of its shaft holds keen-edged cutting bits that can be extended below the base to cut grooves, trim edges, form recesses, produce moldings, and otherwise shape wood on which the router is used.

The power of the router's motor (from ¼ to more than 1 hp in professional models) determines how deep and how fast the tool can cut through work, and what it costs. A low-powered router, however, can do many of the jobs a high-powered router can do, providing it does them in stages. It can make a deep cut, for example, by means of a number of shallow passes.

The router, with its cutter bit operating, may be lowered into the work from above, then moved along the path to be shaped or cut, or it may move into the work from the edge. The bits are set for depth of cut by an adjustment on the router body.

If the bit is to make a large recess, as in a meat platter, it may be mounted on a piece of plywood (large enough to span it from rim to rim) with the cutter projecting downward through a hole in the plywood support. Or you can buy accessories that enable the router to follow templates or guiding edges on the work. With some experience, you will be able to cut designs freehand and even write your name.

As motor shaft, chuck, and bit revolve clockwise (looking down), you should move the tool from left to right. **For safety:** Remember that the router shaft and bit turn at extremely high speed and cut very fast. Be sure the bit is locked tightly in the chuck, and always keep your fingers clear of it. Never change bits or cutters or make adjustments unless the cord is disconnected. Merely switching off the tool is not enough, as switches can be turned on accidentally. Hold the tool firmly on the work when using it, and "feed" from left to right.

To protect the tool, use sharp bits. (They retain their sharpness for a long time in normal use.) Try to get the feel of the most efficient cutting movement. The bit should cut easily with only slight reduction in motor speed. Moving it too slowly through the work may burn the wood and draw the temper of the bit. Moving it too fast slows the motor and causes overheating. Practice on scrap wood and watch performance carefully. The sound of the tool is an ex-

cellent guide, once you achieve efficient cutting. At the beginning, stop the tool frequently and check the cut for burned areas caused by too slow tool movement. Motor slowdown is a signal that you are forcing the cut. The knack usually takes only minutes to acquire. You will find the router especially handy when installing door locks and hinges. In fact, you can buy hinges with rounded corners to match the contour of the opening made by the router bit so that the need for chiseling by hand is eliminated.

When routing narrow work, the base of the router should be extended to gain extra support by fastening a block of wood to the base or to the work.

**Motor:** Oil bearings as shown in owner's manual

**Switch:** Hold router so that it is accessible

**Handles:** Keep clean and grasp firmly

**Adjusting collar:** Lock to desired depth and always make a trial cut first

**Collet:** Keep free of dirt and chips

**Collet nut:** Make sure it is always tight, use wrench supplied

**Base:** Wax occasionally for friction-free movement

**Bit:** Should be sharp and straight

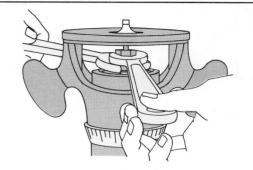

**Inserting router bits:** Disconnect router from power source. You will need two wrenches, unless your router has a locking device that prevents the motor shaft from turning. Hold one wrench on the lower nut and loosen (or tighten) collet nut with upper wrench.

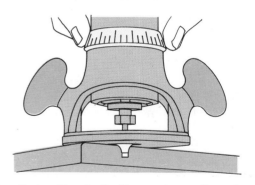

**To adjust cutting depth:** Place router on flat surface. Loosen wing nut and turn collar until bit just touches surface. Lift router and turn collar counterclockwise to lower bit to desired depth; tighten wing nut.

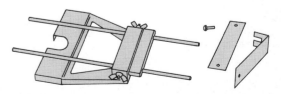

**Router guide,** available for most models, keeps the router bit at the exact desired distance from edge of work. Guide adjusts to and from router base and is held in place by locking screws. Can ride against rim of either straight or curved work as required.

# The router

## Uses of the router

**Grooving:** Use straight bit. Set depth. Adjust router guide or straightedge at desired width. If work is narrow, clamp extra pieces on both sides to make wider base for router.

**Dadoing:** A cut across the width of a board is called a dado. It is used to make slots for shelves. If bit is narrower than desired dado width, make several passes.

**Routing a circular groove:** Mount guide bar to router base. Adjust width. Drill a hole in center of circle. Insert guide pin. Move the router in counterclockwise direction.

**Rabbeting:** Use straight bit. Set depth. If end and edge are to be cut, cut end first (across grain) to prevent edge chipping. Make large rabbets with several passes of bit.

## Router bits and their purposes

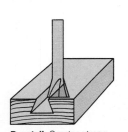

**Dovetail:** Creates strong joints for frames, shelves, bookcases, cabinets.

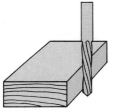

**Spiral:** Edge smoothing and trimming of plastic laminates, fiber glass.

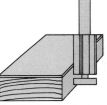

**Combination panel:** Veneer trimming, template panel routing.

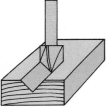

**V-grooving:** Lettering and sign work. Simulates planks on paneling.

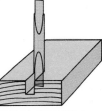

**Straight, single flute:** General stock removal. Grooves, dadoes, rabbets.

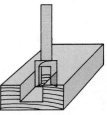

**Stair routing:** Stair tread bit for setting steps and riser grooves.

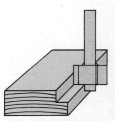

**Rabbeting:** Step-cutting edges for joints in cabinet doors and drawer fronts.

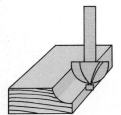

**Cove:** Decorative edges. With matching bit, makes drop-leaf joints.

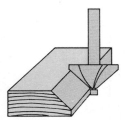

**Chamfering:** Angle cuts for concealed joints and decorative edges.

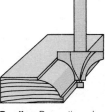

**Beading:** Decorative edges for veneered table tops, other furniture parts.

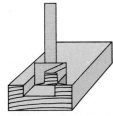

**Straight:** For wood and tile inlay in table tops and various game boards.

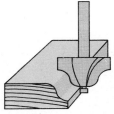

**Roman ogee:** Decorative edges for furniture of different periods.

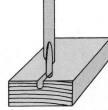

**Veining:** Decorative freehand, raised, or cut-in designs or letters.

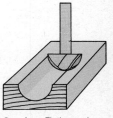

**Core box:** Fluting and reeding of flat surfaces. General ornamentation.

## How to use a bench saw

Today's workshop bench saws (also referred to as table saws or circular saws) range from 7½ to 10 inches in blade diameter, giving them a cutting depth of 1½ to 3⅜ inches. A popular size for average use is 8 inches.

Bench saws can cut long lengths at any width set by the fence, crosscut at any angle set on the miter gauge, and make bevel cuts when the blade is tilted. The blade can be raised or lowered to cut to any depth for grooving. A dado head, used in place of the saw blade, can cut grooves up to ¾-inch wide in a single pass.

The work is always fed to the saw from the front of the table. All settings, such as width, cutting depth, bevel, or miter gauge angle, should be made with the cord unplugged. To make the cut, start the saw and let it reach full speed before pushing in the work. Do not feed the work too fast as it will slow the blade noticeably. (The blade normally slows somewhat while cutting.)

**Safety:** Use the guard for all types of work that permit its use. The guard must be removed for such operations as grooving, coving, and dadoing, and for edge-cutting in wide stock. The photographs on this page have been taken with the guard removed so the operations they show could be seen more clearly. In addition to the guard, it is wise to use goggles when operating the saw. Always stand to one side of the blade, never directly in front of it. Remove your tie and make sure sleeves are snug around your wrists, or else roll them up.

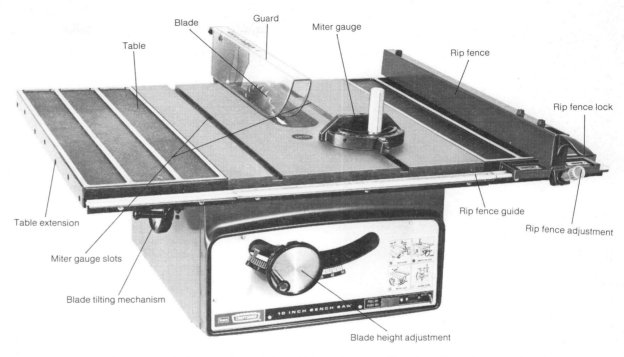

Bench saw is an ideal tool for the workshop with large floor area. Keep the table surface waxed so work will move smoothly into the blade.

**Ripping:** Set the fence for the desired width and hold the work against the fence as you push it through the saw. Do not force it.

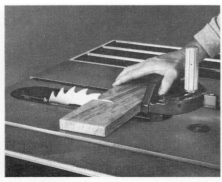

**Crosscutting:** Set the gauge at the desired angle (in this case 90°), hold the work firmly against the gauge, feed slowly.

**When ripping narrow work,** always use a push stick, not your fingers, to feed the work into and through the saw blade.

**Bevel cut** is made by tilting the table to the desired angle. A scale at the tilting mechanism is marked off in degrees.

# Radial arm saw

## How to use a radial arm saw

Guard (shown high for clarity) should always be properly positioned before beginning work. Always keep hands clear of blade. Follow safety instructions in owner's manual.

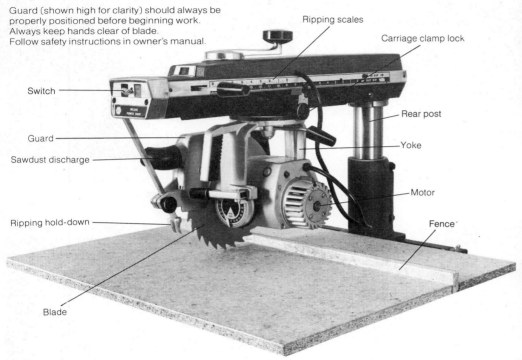

Ripping scales

Carriage clamp lock

Switch

Guard

Sawdust discharge

Rear post

Yoke

Motor

Ripping hold-down

Fence

Blade

Radial arm saw is well suited for smaller workshops. Excellent for crosscutting; can also rip cut. Saw blade can be replaced by an abrasive wheel for grinding applications.

**In crosscutting,** the saw-motor unit is moved toward and across the work. Work is held against the fence.

**To rip,** the saw-motor is locked parallel to the fence at the desired distance and work is pushed through saw.

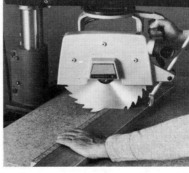

**For an angle cut,** the saw-motor is set at desired angle, work is held against fence, and saw is pulled across work.

**Decorative grooves** are produced by raising blade to make a shallow cut. Dado cut is made with repeated passes.

The radial arm saw does much the same work as the bench saw but cuts from above the work instead of from below. In crosscutting, the radial arm saw has a great advantage over the bench saw. The work is stationary, in fact it can be clamped to the table, while the saw-motor unit moves across the work. This eliminates the awkward procedure of pushing long pieces of lumber across the saw table. The same is true of miter and angle cutting. In ripping, the saw-motor unit is locked parallel to the guide fence, and the work is pushed through the saw, the same as in bench-saw ripping.

**Caution:** When ripping on the radial arm saw, always push the work into the saw from the direction that is indicated on the saw guard, never from the rear.

In cutting completely through the work, the saw blade cuts slightly into the saw table surface (it is nonmetallic, so no harm is done to the blade). This table surface can be replaced when necessary.

The saw-motor unit can be moved in or out along the radial arm in relation to the upright column. The arm can be swung to any desired angle (for mitering or angle cutting), after which the entire assembly is locked in position. As the blade teeth travel away from the table front when crosscutting, the work is set firmly against the replaceable wood fence at the back of the table, and is held there by hand and saw action. In completing a cut, the blade passes through the fence. But as most crosscuts and 45-degree miter cuts follow the same paths, the blade passes through the fence at the original cuts, so that fence replacement is required only at long intervals. Replace the fence with wood the same thickness as the original.

Cutting depth is adjusted by raising the blade instead of lowering it, as on a bench saw. For dado work, remove the blade and install a dado head. For beveling, the saw-motor unit is tipped to the desired angle and locked. The radial arm saw gives the user a clear view of grooving and dado cuts that are concealed by the bench saw. However, because of its more complex design, the radial arm saw is usually higher in price.

## Using rules and tapes

The **folding wood rule** is used for general measuring, especially where its rigidity is needed, as in extending across wide openings like stairwells. The **steel tape rule's** flexibility enables it to measure round as well as straight objects, and its compactness saves space in toolbox or pocket.

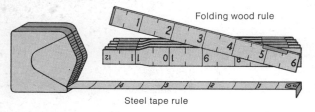

Folding wood rule

Steel tape rule

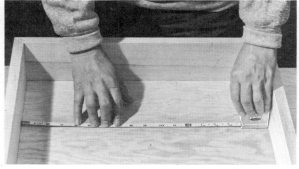

**Inside measurements** can be made with roll-type steel tape if 2 in. are added to compensate for width of tape case.

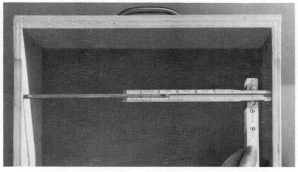

**Open extension-type rule** to nearest section; use slide-out extension for final measurement of inside dimensions.

## Using squares

The **try square** is used to test adjoining surfaces for squareness, mark for right angle cuts. **Combination square** does these jobs and more, including miter marking. **Rafter** or **framing square** is both marking square and carpenter's calculator, scaled so you can mark for rafter cuts according to roof pitch. **T bevel** is used to measure an angle and then transfer it to another area.

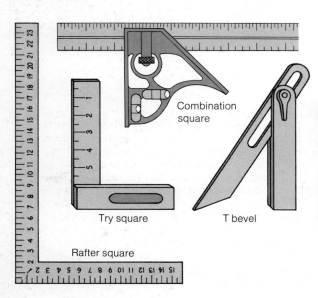

Combination square

Try square

T bevel

Rafter square

**Using combination square** for miter marking: Use other surface of square's body to mark right angles.

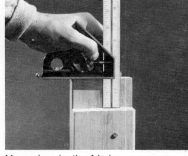

Measuring depth of holes or recesses using combination square: Slide rule-blade into hole; take reading at surface.

Combination square can also be used as a level, a marking gauge, a scribe, and a ruler for measuring and drawing.

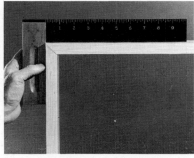

**Use try square** as shown here to test the adjoining surfaces for squareness. Use a plane to square work up, if necessary.

**To mark rafter** or stair stringer cuts along edges of square, set the special scale numbers along edge of lumber.

**To duplicate angle cut,** set T bevel on angle selected, tighten wing nut. Use setting to transfer angle to new work.

# Measuring and marking

## Using levels

Wood, aluminum, or magnesium levels come in lengths to suit their various purposes. Shortest is the **line level,** suspended on taut string for long-span leveling, as in grading or foundation work. Longest is the **mason's level,** usually four feet long. The **carpenter's level** is about two feet long. When the slightly curved bubble tubes, or **vials,** run length-

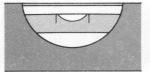

| Bubble position, level | Bubble position, tilted |

wise, they are **level** tubes used for checking horizontal surfaces. Vials that run crosswise are **plumb** for use in checking verticals. Some levels have adjustable vials calibrated from 0 to 90 degrees, for checking pitched surfaces. Others include a 45-degree tube. Select a level that can be read through the top for floor work, and one that can be read through the side for work at or above eye level.

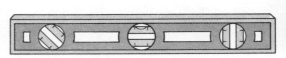

**Carpenter's level** is equipped with both plumb vials for checking vertical surfaces and level vials for checking horizontal surfaces. Made up to 4 ft. long.

**Torpedo level** fits where other models won't. Usually has a top-view level vial and a side-view plumb vial; some are made with a 45° vial as well.

**Line level** is usually about 3 in. long and very light in weight. Hooks at ends hang it on taut string for long-span leveling in grading and foundation work.

**Mason's level** covers broad span in concrete block work, shows which blocks need adjusting while mortar is still fresh.

**Torpedo level:** Handy for checking sill level, angle of miter-positioned trim, level of stationary tools and appliances.

## Tools for marking

The **marking gauge** is used to make a lengthwise scratch on a board for cutting to width. For a pencil mark, use a **combination square,** adjusted to width; slide it along the board edge with pencil held against the blade end. To mark for small circular cuts, use a **wing divider,** available with twin metal points for scratch marking or with point and pencil. For large circular marking, use a pair of **trammel points** mounted on a wood batten. Metal-pointed trammel must be used for center; marking trammel point may have pencil adapter. For very long straight marking, use a **chalk line.**

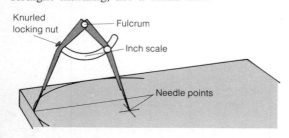

Knurled locking nut — Fulcrum

— Inch scale

Needle points

**Marking gauge is used** to draw a line parallel to the edge of a board at a predetermined distance. Gauge is marked in fractions of an inch. Marker is locked in place with thumbscrew. Some gauges have a brass liner that bears against wood to minimize friction. Hold the gauge at a slight angle as you move it along.

**Trammel points** clamped on a wood batten can be set at the spacing that is required for large circle marking. For scratch marking, use two metal-pointed trammels, one for center, the other for marking. For pencil mark, use one with a pencil holder. Make sure the pencil is sharp and does not wobble in the holder.

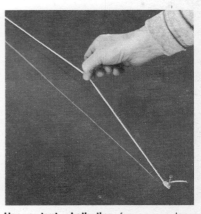

**Use a taut chalk line** for a very long straight-line mark, as in flooring-tile work. Available on reels that apply chalk automatically to line. You simply draw cord taut along the surface where you want the marked line to be, lift it up and snap it back. Chalk marks line. Use two nails as anchors for the chalk line.

## Some basic definitions

Almost all woodworking procedures require some knowledge of simple mathematics, so that tools can be properly set and correct measurements made for the work at hand. The following are a few basic terms necessary for calculating various sizes and shapes, and indispensable to the "working vocabulary" of the home handyman.

**Circumference:** The distance around a circle; the length of the diameter times 3.1416 (pi).

**Diameter:** The distance across a circle through its center; equal to the length of the circumference times .3183.

**Radius:** A straight line from the center of a circle to a point on the circumference or surface.

**Arc:** Part of a curved line, especially a circle.

## Drawing circles

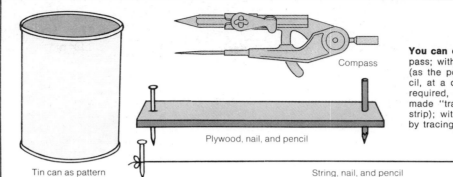

Compass

Plywood, nail, and pencil

Tin can as pattern

String, nail, and pencil

**You can draw a circle:** Using a compass; with a strip of wood and a nail (as the point) at one end and a pencil, at a distance equal to the radius required, at the other (or use ready-made "trammel points" on the wood strip); with a nail, string, and pencil; by tracing a coin, tin can, or plate.

## Calculating sizes and shapes

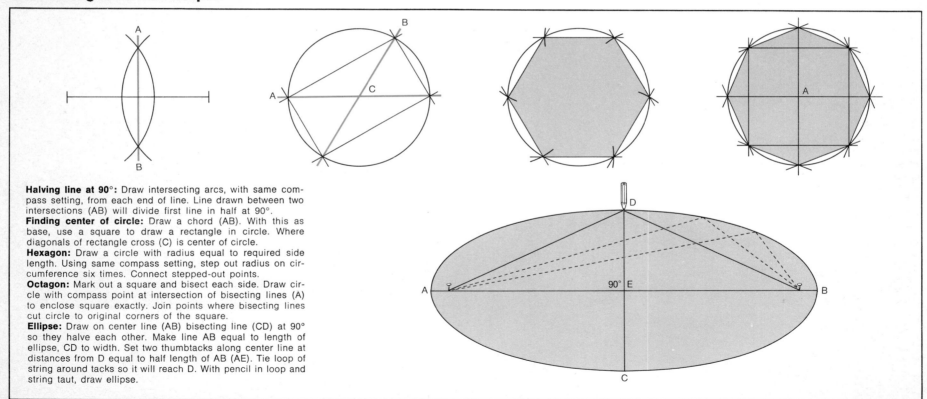

**Halving line at 90°:** Draw intersecting arcs, with same compass setting, from each end of line. Line drawn between two intersections (AB) will divide first line in half at 90°.

**Finding center of circle:** Draw a chord (AB). With this as base, use a square to draw a rectangle in circle. Where diagonals of rectangle cross (C) is center of circle.

**Hexagon:** Draw a circle with radius equal to required side length. Using same compass setting, step out radius on circumference six times. Connect stepped-out points.

**Octagon:** Mark out a square and bisect each side. Draw circle with compass point at intersection of bisecting lines (A) to enclose square exactly. Join points where bisecting lines cut circle to original corners of the square.

**Ellipse:** Draw on center line (AB) bisecting line (CD) at 90° so they halve each other. Make line AB equal to length of ellipse, CD to width. Set two thumbtacks along center line at distances from D equal to half length of AB (AE). Tie loop of string around tacks so it will reach D. With pencil in loop and string taut, draw ellipse.

# Measuring and marking

## Methods of marking angles

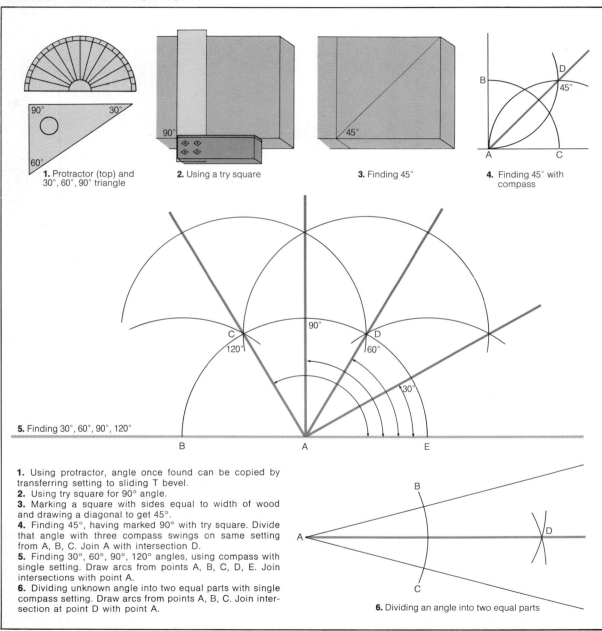

**1.** Protractor (top) and 30°, 60°, 90° triangle

**2.** Using a try square

**3.** Finding 45°

**4.** Finding 45° with compass

**5.** Finding 30°, 60°, 90°, 120°

**6.** Dividing an angle into two equal parts

**1.** Using protractor, angle once found can be copied by transferring setting to sliding T bevel.

**2.** Using try square for 90° angle.

**3.** Marking a square with sides equal to width of wood and drawing a diagonal to get 45°.

**4.** Finding 45°, having marked 90° with try square. Divide that angle with three compass swings on same setting from A, B, C. Join A with intersection D.

**5.** Finding 30°, 60°, 90°, 120° angles, using compass with single setting. Draw arcs from points A, B, C, D, E. Join intersections with point A.

**6.** Dividing unknown angle into two equal parts with single compass setting. Draw arcs from points A, B, C. Join intersection at point D with point A.

## Marking corner curves

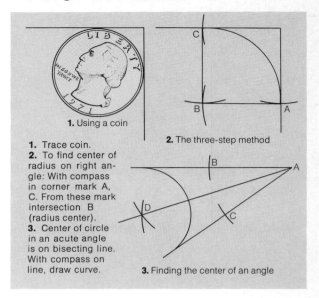

**1.** Using a coin

**2.** The three-step method

**1.** Trace coin.
**2.** To find center of radius on right angle: With compass in corner mark A, C. From these mark intersection B (radius center).
**3.** Center of circle in an acute angle is on bisecting line. With compass on line, draw curve.

**3.** Finding the center of an angle

## Drawing a triangle

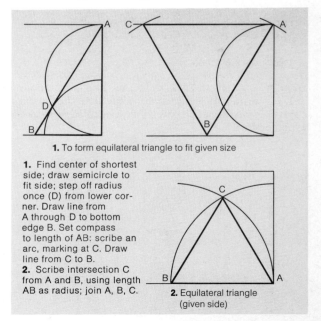

**1.** To form equilateral triangle to fit given size

**1.** Find center of shortest side; draw semicircle to fit side; step off radius once (D) from lower corner. Draw line from A through D to bottom edge B. Set compass to length of AB: scribe an arc, marking at C. Draw line from C to B.
**2.** Scribe intersection C from A and B, using length AB as radius; join A, B, C.

**2.** Equilateral triangle (given side)

## Finding a vertical line

**A spirit level,** used to check surfaces for precise horizontals or verticals, has a bubble in a glass vial with either **one** center mark, or a **pair** of marks separated by a distance equal to the bubble's length. A surface is level (or plumb) in the single-mark type when the bubble is centered; in the two-mark type, when the bubble is between the two. The tubes running crosswise of the level's length are "plumb" vials, used, as

Plumb vial    Level vial    Plumb vial

This level type is good for eye-height use

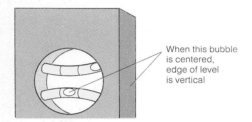

When this bubble is centered, edge of level is vertical

shown in the drawing, to check the accuracy of vertical surfaces.

**By attaching a plumb bob** and line to a board, you can take a vertical line from the board's edge with a pencil. In a 4-x-4-inch board five or six feet long, cut a hole (1) a half-inch longer and two inches wider than the bob (2) and mark a center line on the board (3). Fix a nail into the center line near the board's top (4). Draw a pencil line along board edge to get a true vertical.

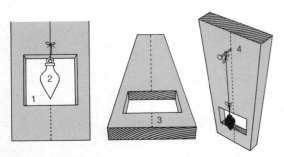

**When using a plumb bob and board** to find a true vertical, make sure that the line swings free of the board.

## Finding a horizontal line

**In using a spirit level** to check a horizontal surface, read the "level" vials—those that run parallel to the level's length. Spirit levels come with extra vials set at 45 degrees for checking certain angular braces. Others include an adjustable protractor dial on one set of vials to give angle readings from 0 to 90 degrees. A line level hangs on a taut string to provide a level line for masonry and other structural work.

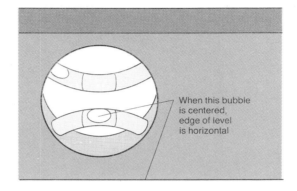

When this bubble is centered, edge of level is horizontal

Combination squares, another option, are described at the right.

**To establish a horizontal without the use of a level,** make a plywood pointer with nail hole at top and point at bottom, both centered. Fix an upright, wider than pointer, to a straightedge and draw a center line through the board at a 90-degree angle to straightedge. Loosely nail pointer to board through center line. Rest straightedge on object to be leveled; move object until pointer aligns with center line.

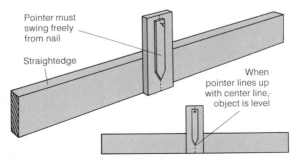

Pointer must swing freely from nail

Straightedge

When pointer lines up with center line, object is level

**Easy-to-make alternative** for a spirit level consists of free-hanging plywood pointer and a board attached to a straightedge.

## Making a straightedge

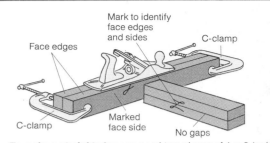

Mark to identify face edges and sides

Face edges

C-clamp

C-clamp

Marked face side

No gaps

**To make a straightedge** you need two pieces of 1-x-3-inch long-planed, straight, even-grained lumber, each four feet long. Hold pieces together, face sides out and face edges together, with a pair of C-clamps. Run a long plane over the butted edges until continual, even, fine shavings appear. Unclamp pieces, place face edges together, and hold up to a strong light. If light shows through the joint, the edges are not true and must be replaned. Mark the gaps and plane as before until edges are true.

## Combination square

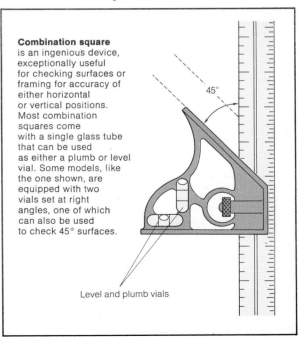

**Combination square** is an ingenious device, exceptionally useful for checking surfaces or framing for accuracy of either horizontal or vertical positions. Most combination squares come with a single glass tube that can be used as either a plumb or level vial. Some models, like the one shown, are equipped with two vials set at right angles, one of which can also be used to check 45° surfaces.

45°

Level and plumb vials

# Deciding what to buy

## Wood grades

There are two basic classifications of lumber: (1) **Select lumber**—excellent quality; for use when appearance and finishing are important; and (2) **common lumber**—has defects; used for construction and general-purpose projects.

The grades of select lumber are: **B and Better grade** (or **1 and 2 clear**)—devoid of any but minute blemishes; **C select grade**—has some minor defects, such as small knots; **D select grade**—has larger imperfections which can be concealed by paint.

The corresponding select grades of Idaho White Pine are designated Supreme, Choice, and Quality.

The grades of common lumber are: **No. 1 grade**—contains tight knots, few blemishes; suitable for natural knotty finish or paint; **No. 2 grade**—has more and larger knots and blemishes; used for flooring and paneling; still suitable for knotty finish or paint; **No. 3 grade**—has loose knots and knotholes and other pronounced flaws; used for shelving, sheathing, fencing, nonvisible purposes; **No. 4 grade**—low quality; used for sheathing, subflooring, crating, and concrete forms; **No. 5 grade**—lowest board grade, for limited use where strength and appearance are not essential to the finished result.

The corresponding grades of Idaho White Pine are Colonial, Sterling, Standard, Utility, and Industrial.

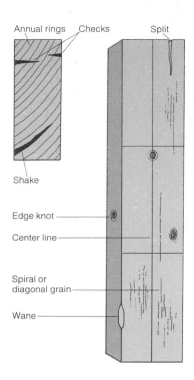

Annual rings · Checks · Split · Shake · Edge knot · Center line · Spiral or diagonal grain · Wane

## Ordering wood

**Board foot,** the unit used in buying lumber, equals the amount of wood in a piece of lumber measuring 1 foot long, 1 inch thick, and 12 inches wide. To calculate the number of board feet, multiply length in feet by **nominal** thickness and width in inches and divide by 12. Thus, the number of board feet in a piece of lumber 6 feet long, 2 inches thick, and 6 inches wide would be:

$$\frac{6 \text{ ft.} \times 2 \text{ in.} \times 6 \text{ in.}}{12} = \frac{72}{12} = 6 \text{ board ft.}$$

**Linear or running foot** is the buying unit for such products as moldings, dowels, furring strips, railings, poles, sometimes 2 x 4s. Length, not thickness or width, is the only consideration. Shingles and laths are usually sold by the bundle, plywood and wallboard by the panel.

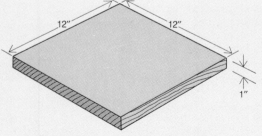

12" · 12" · 1"

Piece of lumber equivalent to board foot

1'

In linear foot, length is only criterion

## Standard sizes

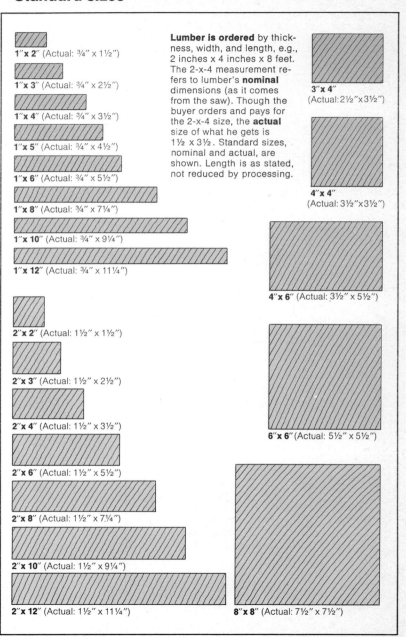

**1″ x 2″** (Actual: ¾″ x 1½″)

**1″ x 3″** (Actual: ¾″ x 2½″)

**1″ x 4″** (Actual: ¾″ x 3½″)

**1″ x 5″** (Actual: ¾″ x 4½″)

**1″ x 6″** (Actual: ¾″ x 5½″)

**1″ x 8″** (Actual: ¾″ x 7¼″)

**1″ x 10″** (Actual: ¾″ x 9¼″)

**1″ x 12″** (Actual: ¾″ x 11¼″)

**2″ x 2″** (Actual: 1½″ x 1½″)

**2″ x 3″** (Actual: 1½″ x 2½″)

**2″ x 4″** (Actual: 1½″ x 3½″)

**2″ x 6″** (Actual: 1½″ x 5½″)

**2″ x 8″** (Actual: 1½″ x 7¼″)

**2″ x 10″** (Actual: 1½″ x 9¼″)

**2″ x 12″** (Actual: 1½″ x 11¼″)

**Lumber is ordered** by thickness, width, and length, e.g., 2 inches x 4 inches x 8 feet. The 2-x-4 measurement refers to lumber's **nominal** dimensions (as it comes from the saw). Though the buyer orders and pays for the 2-x-4 size, the **actual** size of what he gets is 1½ x 3½. Standard sizes, nominal and actual, are shown. Length is as stated, not reduced by processing.

**3″ x 4″** (Actual: 2½″ x 3½″)

**4″ x 4″** (Actual: 3½″ x 3½″)

**4″ x 6″** (Actual: 3½″ x 5½″)

**6″ x 6″** (Actual: 5½″ x 5½″)

**8″ x 8″** (Actual: 7½″ x 7½″)

## How plywood is made

Plywood is made from an odd number of thin sheets of wood, or veneers, glued face to face, with grains running in alternate directions. Lumber core plywood has a solid center ply with thin crisscrossed veneers glued to both its surfaces. Use of an odd number of veneers stabilizes plywood in this way:

If two veneers are bonded together, tensions created by the glue lines, and inherent in the opposite grain directions, will cause warping. But two veneers, each bonded to the opposite sides of a middle panel, will equalize the tension.

New veneers are added in pairs, one on each side, building up to as many as required.

Plywood can still twist, because no two veneers are completely identical and the tensions are never perfectly balanced. Another factor that can cause warping is the wetting or heating of one face of the plywood. This will cause the veneer to expand or contract and may pull the panel out of true.

Plywood for specific uses is factory-processed accordingly. For example, plywood for concrete forms is available with oiled surfaces. Where appearance matters, one or both sides are sanded and natural growth characteristics are repaired.

The most widely used plywoods are softwood types made from fir, pine, and other species and graded according to the quality of the outer plies. Hardwood types include those with all-hardwood veneers and combination types with softwood interiors and hardwood exteriors. Hardwood plywoods (oak, walnut, mahogany, etc.) are generally used only where appearance is a factor.

## Plywood grades

Most plywood made today is graded by the American Plywood Association. Look on the back or along the edges for a stamp bearing the letters APA.

The large capital letters on the grade stamp indicate the quality of the face and back: N (natural finish grade, free of defects, limited repairs); A (smooth and paintable, also usable for less exacting natural finish); B (allows circular repair plugs and tight knots); C (allows knotholes and splits of limited size); D (permits similar flaws, somewhat larger).

The group number indicates the species group used and relative strength ranging from Group 1, the strongest, down to Group 5. Group 1 includes, for example, plywood made from Western larch, loblolly pine, long and short leaf pine, and Douglas fir from Washington, Oregon, California, Idaho, British Co--

Most plywood is cut by placing the log in a giant lathe. As the log turns, a knife slices off a continuous layer of wood, much like peeling the skin from an apple. Most plywood made in the United States and Canada is graded. Look for a stamp at back or edges.

Core    Face    Crossbands

Face

**Lumber-core plywood** is composed of sheets of veneer glued, or laminated, to a middle section of solid wood. It is used in the manufacture of quality furniture.

Face    3- to 9-ply core

Face

**Veneer-core plywood** has a middle section of three to nine or more sheets of veneer, each with its grain set at right angles to those above and below.

— Back veneer
— Crossband
— Lumber core
— Crossband
— Face veneer

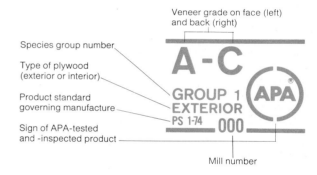

Veneer grade on face (left) and back (right)

Species group number

Type of plywood (exterior or interior)

Product standard governing manufacture

Sign of APA-tested and -inspected product

A-C
GROUP 1  (APA)
EXTERIOR
PS 1-74    000

Mill number

lumbia, and Alberta. Group 2 plywood is made from cedar, Western hemlock, and Douglas fir from Nevada, Utah, and New Mexico. Group 3 comprises plywood made from Alaska cedar, red alder, lodgepole pine, Ponderosa pine, and red, white, and black spruce. Woods used in Group 4 are aspen, paper birch, Western red cedar, Eastern hemlock, sugar pine, and Engelmann spruce. Plywoods in the fifth group include balsam fir and basswood. Other species are included within each group.

The term **Exterior** describing plywood means waterproof glue between plies; **Interior,** moisture-resistant glue, not suited to outdoor or marine use. If there are two additional numbers, such as 48/24, the first indicates maximum spacing between rafters for roof decking, the scond between joists for subflooring. When the second number is zero, as 24/0, the plywood is not suitable for subflooring.

# Wood joints

## Which joint for the job?

This section deals with the variations on basic joints, from the simplest through the more difficult. T joints, for example, start with basic nailed joints and finish with mortise, tenon, and dovetail joints. Joints can be divided into six groups:

**T joints:** One piece joined at right angles to the face or edge of another, forming a T shape.

**L joints:** Two pieces joined to form a corner.

**X joints:** The pieces crossed over or fixed into each other to form a cross.

**Edge (-to-edge) joints:** Edges that are joined to produce wider surfaces.

**Lengthening joints:** Two pieces joined end to end.

**Three-way joints:** Three pieces of wood joined; e.g., a chair leg and rails.

## Nailed T joints

Simple nailed joints are satisfactory for light frames where the sides meet the crosspieces squarely. Be sure the butt ends of the crosspieces are square and the sidepieces are smooth. Otherwise the joint cannot form a true right angle.

Use three nails: Hammer the middle one in first to hold the wood firm, then drive in the other two on either side of it, sloping them inward at angles of 20 to 30 degrees. These nails form a dovetail.

Toe nailing from the inside of a frame requires care. Hammer from both sides alternately and re-align the work as the nail points bite into the sidepiece. Drive nails in line with the grain, but stagger them to avoid splitting.

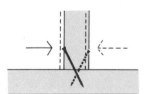

Take care that wood does not move as you hammer

Set the nailheads below the surface of the wood for extra tightness. Fill holes with filler or putty.

Use finishing nails on trim and exposed work, common nails on structural framing. The nail length should be at least three times the thickness of the wood through which it is driven.

## Using braces and fasteners

Metal braces and mending plates are helpful in making flat T joints. There are four types: One, known as an **inside corner brace,** is a strip of drilled metal bent into a simple L shape for fitting into corners; another, called a **T plate,** is a flat T shape, and screws flat onto the work. The **flat corner plate** is similar, but L shaped, for corner use. The **mending plate** is straight, for straight line reinforcement.

Use these whenever the appearance and thickness of the brace do not matter, as in light framing, which needs a little more strength than nailed joints would provide, also for repairs. Obviously, the stronger the brace the stronger the joint, but, in some applications, the braces will bend unless you use one on each side of the joint.

The screws should fit the drilled holes snugly. Drill pilot holes in the wood to prevent splitting. Drive the screws home flush with the top.

A far quicker way to make T joints (where high strength isn't required) is with corrugated metal fasteners which are hammered straight into the work. These fasteners are sharpened on one edge. They are best used on light indoor work, such as screen frames and box-making.

Make sure that the joint is as tight as possible before you drive the fasteners home.

Position the fasteners well in from the edges of the crosspiece to prevent splits. Tap gently until they are going in evenly, then hammer them along the top until they are flush with the surface.

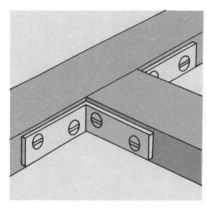

**Two corner braces** prevent bending

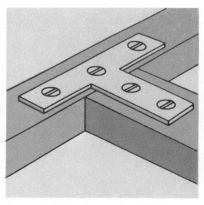

**Screw T plates** flat on the surface

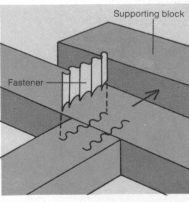

**Hammer in** corrugated fasteners

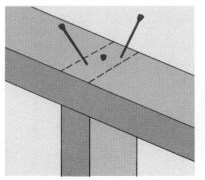

**Direct nailing:** Two-thirds of the nail length should be in the crosspiece.

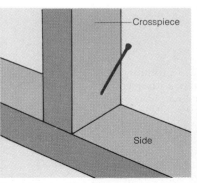

**Toe nailing:** Drive nails from opposite sides at about a 30° angle.

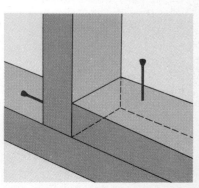

**A block** may be nailed to one member to receive nails driven through the other.

## Overlap joints

The overlap T joint is used for general-purpose jobs. It can be secured by screws, nails, or bolts, and, for strongest results, may also be glued.

To make a strong screwed-overlap joint, clamp both pieces of wood together with a C-clamp (p. 12). Drill a clearance hole through the top piece and a pilot hole in the lower piece, using a bit small enough for the screw thread to bite firmly. Countersink holes in top piece, coat inner surfaces with glue, fit pieces together, then drive screw home.

A simple glued-and-screwed T joint, combined with supporting blocks, produces sturdy shelving units. Glue and screw blocks to each side of the casing, then glue and screw the shelving to the blocks.

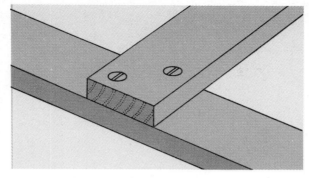

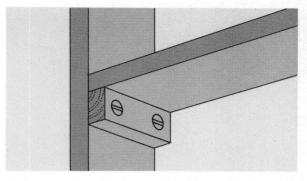

**Overlap T joint:** Screw diagonally to avoid splitting wood

**Shelf support:** Screw block to upright; screw in shelves

## Full and half lap joints

Use these strong, neat joints for fitting crossrails flush into frames to be paneled.

In a **full lap joint** the side rail is cut out to accommodate the whole of the crossrail. To make it, mark the exact shape of the cutout on both faces of the side rail and across its top edge.

Cut out the waste gradually from each side with a backsaw and chisel until the base of the cutout is level. Check the fit, glue all mating surfaces, and complete the joint by nailing or screwing.

In a **half lap joint,** the crossrail and the side rail are both cut away to give a flush fit when they are mated.

Mark the width of the crossrail across the face of the side rail and halfway down both edges.

On the back of the crossrail, mark a shoulder line across at a distance from the end a little greater than the width of the side rail.

Continue the line halfway across the edges. Set a marking gauge to half the thickness of the wood and gauge lines from the face of both pieces.

Saw a center slot in the crossrail, skimming the gauge line on the waste side. Remove the waste block by cutting across the shoulder line.

Saw just inside the lines marking the side rail cutout. Saw an extra cut in the center to make waste removal easier. Using a chisel, remove the waste from both sides to complete the cutout, check for fit, fix, and trim. If you have difficulty assembling the pieces, sand the leading edges lightly. If the joint is to be glued, use the glue sparingly.

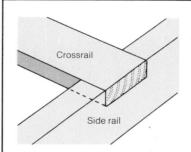

**Full lap joint:** Set in flush with the face of a frame, joint provides strength as well as a neat look.

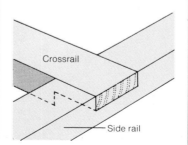

**Half lap joint:** Quick and simple method of joining wood of equal thickness. Glue and nail the pieces together for greater strength.

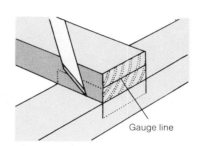

Gauge line

**1.** To make the half lap joint, mark off the width of the crossrail. Keep the pieces perpendicular to each other.

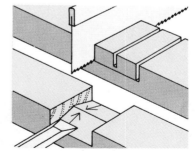

**3.** Make three backsaw cuts—one on each side of the cutout and one in the middle. Chisel the waste away from both sides down to the gauge lines.

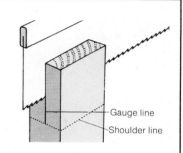

Gauge line

Shoulder line

**2.** Next saw down the center of the crossrail, skimming the gauge line on the waste side.

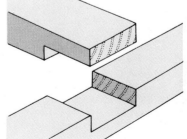

**4.** The finished joint should tap together easily. Make sure the shoulders are secure. Glue and nail. Allow the glue to set, then trim.

# Dado joints

## Plain and stopped dadoes

The dado joint is the classic way of joining the end or edge of one board into the cut surface of another. There are two principal types: The **plain dado,** in which the cutout continues all the way across the joining member, and the **stopped dado,** in which the dado extends only part way.

Both types can be dovetailed by cutting one side of the housing and the matching edge of the cross member at an inward sloping angle (p. 37).

The stopped dado is the type that is used for display and cabinet work.

**Making the joint:** First, mark a line at right angles across the inner face of the piece to be dadoed. Hold the cross member against the line and draw a line along its other side to give the exact width of the dado.

Continue these lines across both edges of the upright. Mark the depth of the dado—usually it is one-third of the wood thickness from the face side of both edges.

Cut down carefully to depth on both sides of the housing with a backsaw.

Chisel away the waste from each edge. Start with a sloping cut and gradually reduce the paring angle until the center is chiseled away. Finish the cut with a hand router.

If you do not have a hand router available, take extra care with the paring and check frequently with a straightedge for depth and flatness. The dado can also be cut on a table or radial arm saw, using a dado set in place of the blade and setting it for the width and depth of the cut (this is the easiest way).

**The stopped dado joint:** Construction is similar to that of the regular joint except that the cutout ends a short distance from the front edge (or edges) of the dadoed member. The corner of the inserted member is cut away to overlap this distance.

Mark as usual for the joint but also mark the stopped end (or ends) of the dado from the edge.

To make space for a saw, chisel out a recess from the stopped end to near the correct depth. Saw to depth from the unstopped edge on both sides. Chisel away the waste and clean out to depth with a router. If both ends are stopped, cut the dado with a chisel, or with a router.

On the inserted member, mark the cutout to depth and length and cut away the corners for the overlap. Saw away the waste with a backsaw.

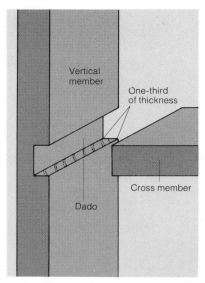

**Dado joint:** A clean, strong joint. The cross member takes considerable weight and is ideal for bookshelves.

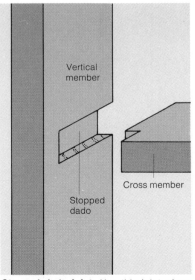

**Stopped dado joint:** Use this joint where appearance matters. Overlap neatly conceals its construction on the front.

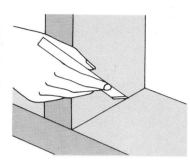
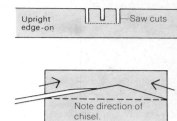

**To make a dado joint:** Place cross member against a squared line on the inner face of the upright and mark on other side for the exact cut.

After sawing to depth, gradually chisel out the waste from each edge until the center is completely removed. Then trim to depth.

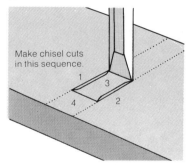
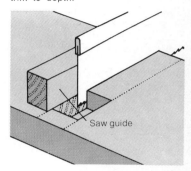

Make chisel cuts in this sequence.

**To make a stopped dado joint:** Make room for saw movement by chiseling a recess at stopped end of joint.

On long cuts, run the saw against a guide batten that is temporarily clamped to the work.

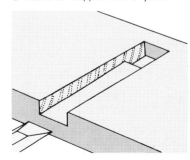
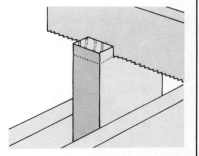

Chisel out waste, then finish cut with hand router or paring chisel.

Saw off cut-away corner on cross member to the depth of the housing.

## Making the basic joint

The strongest of the T joints, used for heavy framing and in general furniture work. The thickness of the tenon should not exceed one-third the thickness of the mortised member.

To make the joint, mark the width of the member to be tenoned **(rail)** on the member to be mortised **(stile)** and continue the lines as a guide. On the ends of the mortise outline, mark lines for wedges—about ⅛ inch outside existing lines—if joint is to be wedged. Square a shoulder line right around the member to be tenoned, to give a tenon length just greater than the mortise depth.

Select your chisel and set mortise limit points to its width. (You may use a regular marking gauge by resetting it after first marking.) Center the mortise

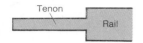

Tenon
Rail

Tenon thickness: One-third of stock

(for methods, see p. 27), then cut back to edge lines on outer edge. You can speed the mortise by boring through at each end with an auger bit, then chiseling between holes. Saw down tenon line faces and cut carefully across at shoulder lines.

Apply glue, assemble, clamp, and hammer in glued wedges. Sand off protrusions when glue has set.

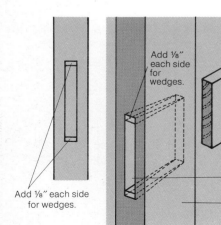

Add ⅛" each side for wedges.

Add ⅛" each side for wedges.

Tenon

Rail

Mortise

Stile

**Marking out:** Make tenon long enough to project slightly beyond mortise.

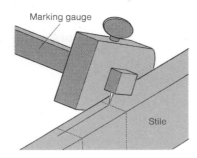

Marking gauge

Stile

**1.** Set the point of the marking gauge for the outside limit of the mortise to be cut in the rail.

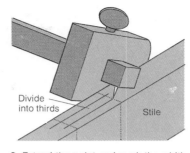

Divide into thirds

Stile

**2.** Extend the point and mark the width of the mortise. Make it equal to one-third the total thickness of the wood.

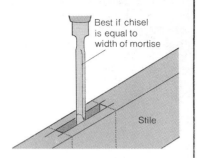

Best if chisel is equal to width of mortise

Stile

**3.** Cut out the mortise, working from both sides until recesses meet. Trim out, then cut back for wedges.

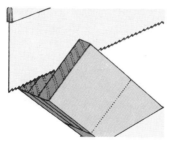

**4.** Make sloping cuts down both tenon lines alternately from each edge. Skim the lines on the waste side.

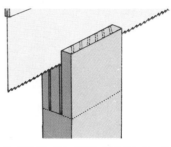

**5.** Clamp the work upright in vise, then saw the waste down squarely to the shoulder lines.

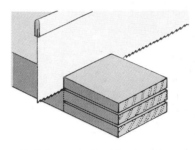

**6.** Cut across shoulder lines to complete tenon, making sure the saw is straight. Fit tenon into mortise.

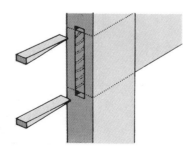

**7.** Apply glue to the tenon and inside the mortise. Fit the parts together. Cut finely tapered wedges to fit part way into the ⅛-in. slots at the ends of the mortise.

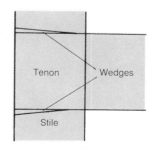

Tenon          Wedges

Stile

**8.** Apply glue to the wedges and drive them into the slots. Hammer both in at the same time, striking them alternately to keep tenon straight in mortise. Clamp the assembly.

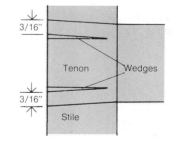

3/16"

Tenon          Wedges

3/16"

Stile

**9.** Another wedging method is to saw wedge slots about two-thirds down the length of the tenon, 3/16 in. in from the edges. The wedges jam the tenon into the shape of the mortise.

# Mortise and tenon joints

## Variations on the basic joint

The mortise and tenon joint strengthens furniture construction and provides a pleasing appearance. Extra shoulders may be cut, reducing the width of the tenon by ⅛ to ½ inch top and bottom to completely hide the ends of the mortise slot.

**Rabbeted or haunched tenon:** A very strong joint for window frames, doors, and furniture. It can be used as an L joint—on corners—as well as a T joint. The haunch can be sloping, instead of square as

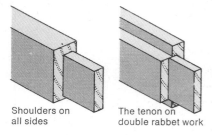

Shoulders on all sides    The tenon on double rabbet work

shown. The haunch resists twisting, but does not weaken the stile, as a full width tenon would.

Proportions are important. Make the mortise and tenon about one-third the thickness of the wood—if too wide, the joint will be weakened.

Make the length of the haunch not more than one-third the length of the tenon. Its depth should be no more than a quarter of the width of the mortised member, or ½ inch—whichever measurement is the smaller. Often the depth is determined by a groove in the frame.

Leave at least ½ inch of waste on the end of the mortised member to prevent splitting while making and fitting the joint. Trim when the glue sets.

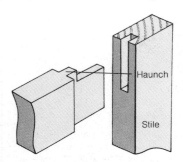

Haunch

Stile

Make the haunch one-third the length of the tenon

**Double tenon:** Use a double tenon where a single tenon would be so wide as to weaken the upright.

The joint has great resistance to twisting where extra-wide rails have to be fitted to uprights. Set it out and cut the same as for a single tenon.

**Stub tenon:** This joint serves much the same purpose as the plain mortise and tenon, but the tenon in this type is stopped short so that it does not appear on the outside.

The depth of the mortise should be about two-thirds the width of the wood. Cut the tenon about ⅛ inch short of this depth measurement. This will

keep it from touching the bottom of the mortise.

**Scribed tenon:** The scribed tenon is used on work in which one or both edges have molding, such as window frames.

Cut the tenoned piece oversize by the depth of the molding. Then, with a chisel, cut away the shoulders of the tenon to match the molding on the other member. Trim to fit.

**Twin mortise and tenon:** This joint is mainly used on the center rail, or lock rail, of door frames. The divided tenons span the lock, which is mortised from the outside.

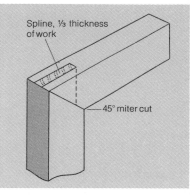

**Open mortise and tenon:** Easy to make, and strong using modern resin glues.

Glue and clamp, sand when dry

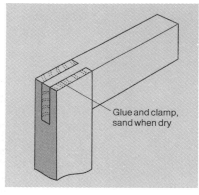

**Miter with feather joint** locked by square spline fitted into outer corner of joint.

Spline, ⅓ thickness of work

45° miter cut

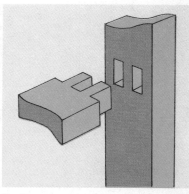

**Double tenon** should have tenon widths the same as the gaps between them.

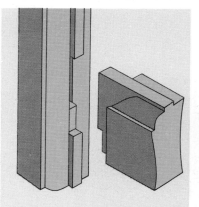

**Scribed tenon,** used where moldings meet; tenon shoulders match joining part.

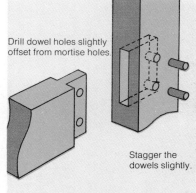

Drill dowel holes slightly offset from mortise holes.

Stagger the dowels slightly.

**Stub tenon** runs part way through; may be locked with staggered dowels plus glue.

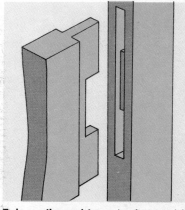

**Twin mortise and tenon** is often used for wide rail of door at lock location.

## Single dovetail

The single dovetail is a mechanically strong joint for furniture rails that have to bear weight.

To construct it, first mark out and cut the pin (this is the flared projection at the end of the rail or board) with either a backsaw or a dovetail saw (2). Make the angle of the pin 1:6 for softwood (1) and 1:8 for hardwood.

Transfer the pin shape to the other frame piece (3) by marking with a pencil or knife.

Saw down the shoulders of the dovetail cutout and make an extra cut in the center of the waste to facilitate chiseling work (4). Put joint together dry (before gluing) to check for fit (5). Then glue and clamp (6), wiping off excess glue to reduce required sanding later.

The same type of single dovetail can also be cut very quickly with a jigsaw that has a tilt adjustment. Use the saw with the blade in vertical position to cut the pin. Then mark the shape of the pin on the second piece. Cut this part of the joint by adjusting the table tilt to the marked joint angle and cutting inward from the edge. Use a chisel to separate the waste piece between cuts.

Small dovetails and multiple types, as in drawer corners, can be cut rapidly with a router, using a dovetail bit. If a dovetail attachment is available for the router, as is the case with many models, a complete drawer-corner dovetail can be cut in about one minute, as both parts are cut simultaneously by the dovetail-shaped bit.

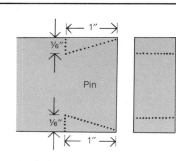

**1.** Mark both of the dovetail parts for cutting. Cut on the waste side, then trim.

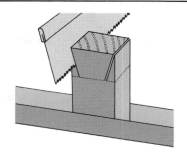

**2.** Cut the dovetail with a fine-toothed backsaw or saber saw for smoothness.

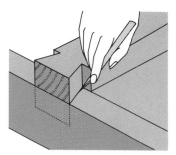

**3.** Mark the cut dovetail on the mating part of the joint for precise cutting.

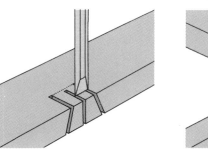

**4.** Cut the second part with a backsaw or saber saw. Chisel out the waste wood.

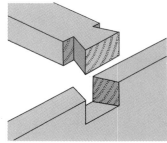

**5.** Fit the joint parts together dry to check fit. Trim them before applying the glue.

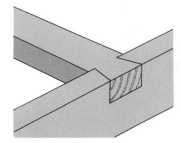

**6.** Glue and clamp the joint, wiping off any excess glue to reduce amount of sanding.

## L joints: Six ways to make corners

Six corner joining methods are shown on the right. Wooden blocks can be square or triangular in cross section. Triangular ones (1) are neater.

The strength of glued joints depends mainly on the glue, though screws or dowels can reinforce them. Hammer the nails home dovetail-fashion. Stagger the dowels or screws to avoid splitting. Make sure the dowels or screws do not meet in the middle. Metal reinforcements can either be screwed to the top and bottom of the corner (4) or screwed only on the inside of the joints (5). The first method is the stronger.

Triangular plywood gussets (6), or glue blocks, at top and bottom, are glued and bradded to the corner. Trim outside edges when glue is dry.

| **1** | **2** | **3** | **4** | **5** | **6** |
|---|---|---|---|---|---|

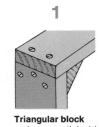 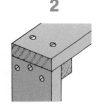  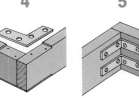 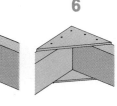

**Triangular block** makes smooth inside corner in cabinet-work. Has same glue grip as square block.

**Square block** allows greater depth for screws. Often used where appearance is not essential.

**Outside glue block** permits screw fastening where unobstructed inner corners are needed.

**Flat corner plates** recessed into edges at corners produce a strong joint with minimum effort.

**Inside corner braces** do job when edges must be smooth, as when plywood will be attached.

**Plywood gussets** and triangular pieces make a very rigid joint when nailed and glued.

# Dovetail variations

## Through dovetail

The through dovetail is the strongest and most decorative of the corner joints. It is used extensively for backs of drawers and in general cabinetwork.

Assemble the wood to be joined, marking the matching pieces forming the corners. Plane the end true and square, allowing $\frac{1}{16}$ inch for overall waste. Set the marking gauge to the wood thickness plus $\frac{1}{32}$ inch (the allowance for waste on each corner). Mark gauge line (a) on all sides and edges.

Use a dovetail template (angles 1:6 for softwoods; 1:8 for hardwoods) to mark the dovetails. Square the lines across the ends.

Cut down the dovetails with a backsaw (1); remove the waste with a coping saw (2); trim out with a chisel (3).

Use the dovetails as patterns to mark out the pins on the ends of the side pieces (4). Saw along the marked lines (5); remove the waste with a coping saw; then trim with a chisel.

Save time when making several joints by cutting all the dovetails at once with the dovetail pieces clamped together in the vise.

Test the joints for fit (6). Do this with the parts dry in case further trimming is needed; if all is well, glue and clamp.

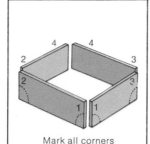

Mark all corners

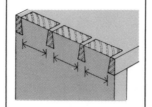

Space pins evenly

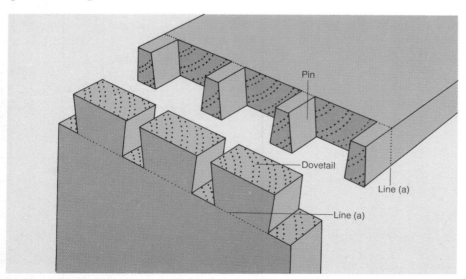

**Marking out dovetails:** The dovetails give the greatest strength when positioned at both sides of drawers, packing boxes, and upright frames.

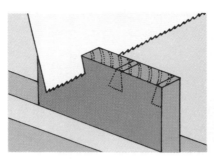

**1.** Cut the dovetails in the vise with a backsaw. Saw within the waste.

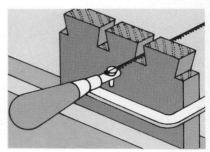

**2.** Remove the bulk of the waste with a coping saw. Take care not to saw into the dovetails. Hold the saw level.

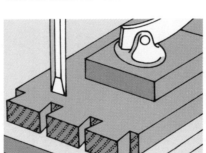

**3.** Trim out the socket, using a narrow chisel. Keep the work steady by securing it with a clamp.

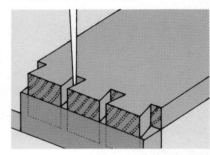

**4.** Mark out the pins, using a sharp pencil or the front tooth of the saw.

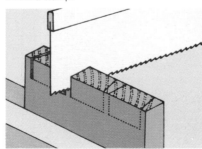

**5.** Saw down the pin lines, then remove the waste with a coping saw. Trim out with the largest possible chisel.

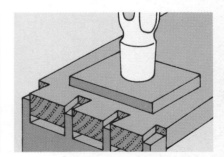

**6.** The completed joint should fit firmly when tapped in place. Use a spare block so the hammer won't damage the surface. Position the pins at the top and bottom on frames, at the back for drawers.

## Lap, double-lap, and secret dovetails

The lap dovetail is used where the ends of the dovetails would spoil the appearance of the work.

Cut and plane the side to the length of the drawers, less the thickness of the lap (⅛ inch on ¾-inch wood, a proportion of 1:6). Cut and plane the front to the size of the opening it must fit.

Set the cutting gauge to the thickness of the front, less ⅛ inch for the lap. Gauge line (a) on the end of the front and on the inside and line (b) all around the end of the side, with the cutting gauge at the same setting. Mark the dovetails as for the common dovetail and cut the same way.

Butt the tails against line (a) on the front and mark off the shape of the pins.

Mark the depth of the pins on the inside of the front. Saw the pins at 45 degrees, with wood held upright in the vise. Chop out the waste, keeping the chisel short of line (a) until the bulk is removed.

The overhang of the pins prevents cutting straight into their corners. Ease out the waste at these points with a narrow chisel.

Trim the inner faces of the pins by paring them with a chisel. Finally, run a groove for the drawer bottom through a dovetail so that it will be covered by the lap.

Variations on the joint are the **double-lap dovetail,** and the **secret,** or **miter dovetail.**

In both the double-lap and the miter dovetail joints, cut the pins first.

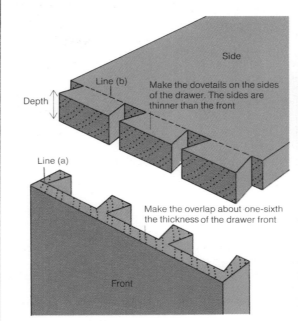
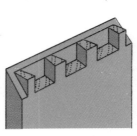

Line (b)

Side

Make the dovetails on the sides of the drawer. The sides are thinner than the front

Depth

Line (a)

Front

Make the overlap about one-sixth the thickness of the drawer front

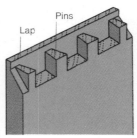
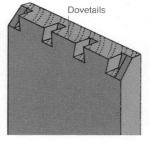

Lap

Pins

Dovetails

**Double-lap dovetail** shows only a small amount of end grain. It is neat, but demands care in construction. It incorporates miters at corners and provides a strong joint.

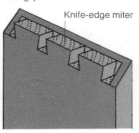

Knife-edge miter

**Lap dovetail** is the ideal joint for the fronts of drawers and the corners of bookcases. Cut the dovetails in the sides and the pins in the overlapping pieces.

**Secret, or miter, dovetail** is an uncommon joint used chiefly for quality work. It takes practice to achieve the undamaged knife-edge that gives the miter a perfect fit.

**Cutting the lap** on a lap dovetail joint requires, first, that you place the dovetail side piece on top of the front piece, then use the saw cuts, as shown, to mark the pins.

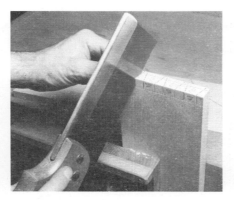

Hold the front piece upright in the vise and saw down the pins at 45° as far as possible. Be careful not to saw into the lap. The waste area should be clearly marked.

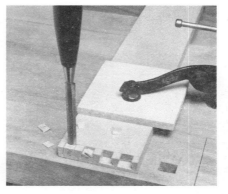

The next step is cutting out the waste. Be very careful as you work to keep the chisel always well back from the gauge line until most of the waste has been removed.

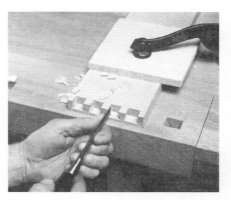

Use a very narrow chisel to trim the corners covered by the overhang of the pins. It is recommended that you secure the wood with a clamp during this part of the operation.

# Right-angle joints

## Rabbeted and grooved joints

You can simplify drawer construction and other projects normally requiring dovetailed corners by substituting rabbeted or grooved joints. They are quick to make and strong enough for most jobs.

Allow a little extra length on the front so that you can make the rabbet slightly wider than the thickness of the wood it joins. This allows for final cleaning up. The depth of the rabbet should be not more than three-quarters the thickness of the wood it joins.

Cut the rabbet with a backsaw or on a power saw with a dado attachment. Glue and nail the joint. Nail the brads in opposite directions.

Use this joint on the front corners of drawers with the rabbet overlapping the sides.

For drawer fronts that extend beyond the sides, use a groove and rabbet joint. Cut the groove in the inner face of the drawer front and the rabbet on the inner face of the side. Both groove and rabbet can be dovetail-shaped for extra strength.

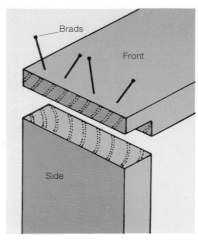

**Rabbet joint:** First make the horizontal cut, then the vertical; use a back saw.

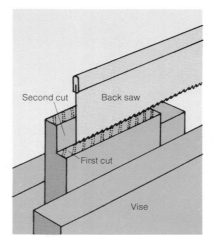

Check fit, apply glue; nail brads in opposing directions for added strength.

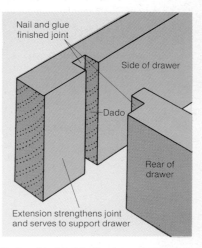

**Dado-rabbet joint:** Overhang strengthens joint, gives support to extended drawer.

## Bridle and box joints

A bridle or a finger (box) joint is strong but needs to be well made for a pleasing effect. Both are ideal for such jobs as joining legs to chair arms.

Use the bridle joint at a corner—where it becomes an open mortise and tenon—or at a T joining, where it is more decorative than a plain half lap joint. For both types, divide the edge of the work into thirds. Square off the shoulder lines on both pieces and mark the finger and cutout lines from the face sides.

Mark the waste wood clearly with Xs so that there will be no mistakes. Saw down the cutout section, skimming the gauge lines in the waste. Remove most of the waste by cutting across near the bottom with a coping saw. Next, square off at the shoulder line with a narrow chisel.

Cut the finger of a corner joint as you would a tenon. On the through joint, cut out from both sides. Saw down to the gauge marks and chisel out the waste from both sides.

Both joints can be strengthened with dowels. To get extra tightness, offset the dowel holes slightly so that the dowel, when driven home, forces the finger against the bottom of the cutout.

The box, comb, or finger joint is machine-made as a general rule, but it can be made by hand as an alternate to dovetailing on light furniture and in box construction.

One of the pieces must contain two end fingers, so the total number of fingers will be uneven.

Score each shoulder with a knife. Darken to make the lines clearer and mark off the waste. Check one piece against the other before you cut the joint.

In the construction of these joints, follow the axiom of measuring twice and cutting once. It's easy to correct an error on paper; wood is another story.

All of the joints described should be reinforced with brads and white glue. When making a drawer, be sure it will fit the opening it is designed for with adequate clearance all around.

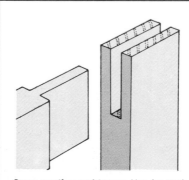

**Open mortise and tenon:** Use for such jobs as joining legs to chair arms.

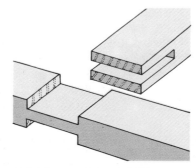

**T joining or through bridle:** Better appearance than plain half lap joint.

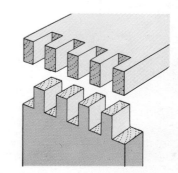

**Box joint:** Has many uses in construction of light furniture and drawers.

## Four ways to make miter joints

Miter joints are used for picture frames and larger jobs such as bookcases. The miter angle of 45 degrees must be cut and trimmed accurately. It must also be strengthened in one of several ways.

The simplest method is to glue both surfaces, then clamp the corner in a vise (use padding). This prevents the hammer from knocking the joint out of shape. Nail the brads home in opposite directions and fill the holes.

A stronger method is to saw slots dovetail-fashion across the outer edge of the corner, with both pieces held together in a vise. Insert "keys" of veneer and trim when the glue dries.

Splined or tongued miters are even stronger. Avoid damaging the edge of the miter by making a 45-

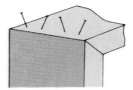

Nailing a miter joint

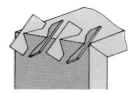

Using veneer in slots

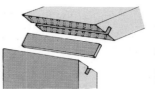

Spline reinforces miter

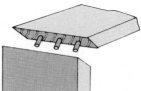

Doweled miter joints

degree block the same width as the work. Clamp the block and the work together in a vise and cut the groove, using the block as a guide. Cut the tongue from stiff plywood.

Doweling is effective, but the holes need careful drilling. Locate them exactly by tapping brads at the

dowel positions in one miter face. Cut the brads and drill both sets of holes at right angles to the miter. Set the holes nearer the inner work face to allow for a reasonable length of dowel.

A necessity for making accurate miter joints is a well-constructed miter box and backsaw.

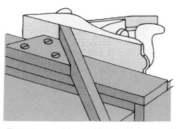

**1.** Cut the miter carefully in a miter box using a backsaw. Make sure molding faces the right way before cutting.

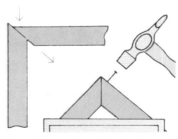

**2.** Trimming with a plane shortens the work, so allow about ½₂ in. for this when sawing the miter. Trim to exact length with plane on miter board. Make sure plane is sharp; give it a fine setting.

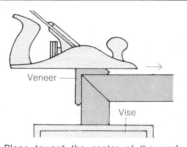

**3.** If possible, nail a mitered corner with the joint held firmly in a vise to prevent the hammer knocking it out of line.

**4.** Plane toward the center of the work when trimming veneer that is set into the corners.

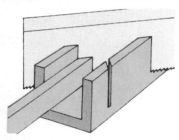

**5.** Use a 45° block the same width as the work as a guide for cutting a groove for a spline across a miter.

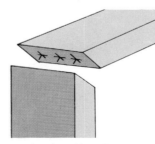

**6.** Locate dowel positions by temporarily nailing brads into one face. Cut them off short and make their impressions on the other face. Remove the brads and exact positions for all dowels are marked. Use depth gauge when drilling.

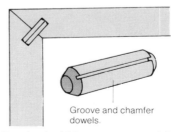

**7.** Dowels should have a groove cut the long way to let glue escape. Chamfer the ends so they will fit into the holes easily. Coat the dowels with white glue.

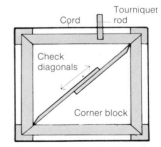

**8.** Pull a mitered frame tight with a cord running around corner brackets and tightened with a turnbuckle. Check the diagonals—they should be equal.

# X or crisscross joints

## Five ways to make them

The simplest of the X joints is the plain overlap. Held together with glue and screws for greatest strength, it can also be bolted, clinch-nailed, glued and doweled, or glued and nailed.

The cross-lap—one of the easiest and most useful of the various joints—is cut in the same way as the half lap joint. Whether it is made flat or on edge, the eggcrate construction is the same. Glue and clamp the pieces together firmly. Trim the joint when the glue is thoroughly dry.

By reducing the depth of the cutout, one rail can be made to project over the other.

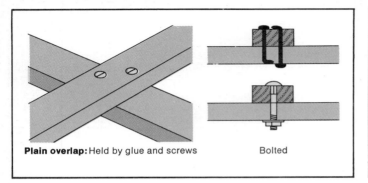

**Plain overlap:** Held by glue and screws

Bolted

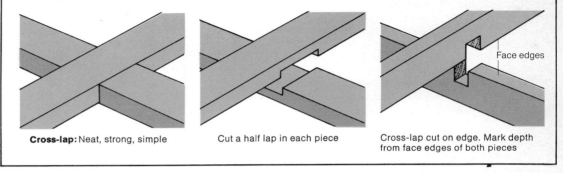

**Cross-lap:** Neat, strong, simple

Cut a half lap in each piece

Cross-lap cut on edge. Mark depth from face edges of both pieces

Face edges

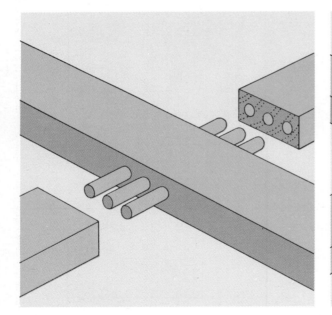

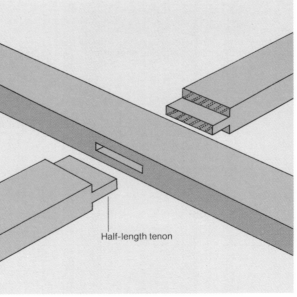

Half-length tenon

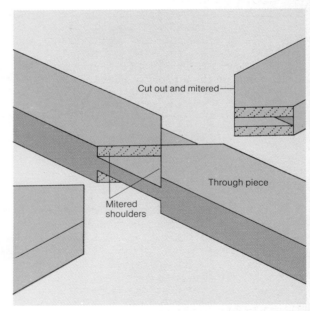

Cut out and mitered

Through piece

Mitered shoulders

**Doweled joint:** Make an X joint on a heavy frame by using dowels and drilling out with a doweling jig. This joint has many advantages. It has more strength than a nailed joint, is neater, and is relatively easy to construct.

**Mortise-tenon joint:** An alternate method of making a strong and attractive X joint is to cut a mortise on the through piece and half-length tenons on the joining rails. Then glue and clamp the pieces together.

**Mitered bridle joint:** Mark the edges as for the bridle joint and scribe miter lines across all faces. Work to a fine point in the center of the through piece by cutting each of the mitered shoulders individually.

## Edge-to-edge joint

Edge-to-edge joints are used when it is necessary to increase the width of lumber for table tops or for wide shelving. There are three methods of making them: Gluing, doweling, and loose-tongue (or spline) joining.

Before joining, the boards must be planed to a perfect edge-to-edge match. Preparatory to planing, clamp both boards together with the edges to be joined uppermost. Then, using a jointer plane (p. 7), plane both edges at once until they seem to the eye to be flat and even.

Check the result for accuracy by holding the planed edges together. No daylight should show through at any point if they are evenly planed.

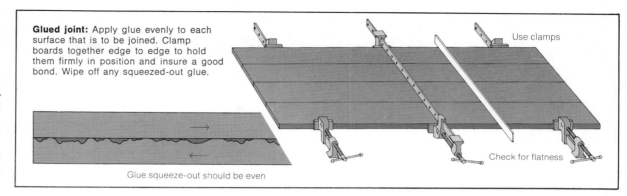

**Glued joint:** Apply glue evenly to each surface that is to be joined. Clamp boards together edge to edge to hold them firmly in position and insure a good bond. Wipe off any squeezed-out glue.

Use clamps

Check for flatness

Glue squeeze-out should be even

## Dowel joint

A dowel jig insures the needed accuracy for this joint. Plane the edges straight and square.

Mark the dowel locations by clamping both boards back to back; square lines across to allow for one dowel every six or nine inches. Intersect marks with a central gauge line from each face side (1).

Drill holes, checking often for squareness. Use a depth gauge on the bit to give a hole slightly deeper than half the dowel length (2).

Chamfer the dowels at each end to aid location in assembly. Saw a groove along each dowel to allow trapped glue to escape. Glue and insert the dowels in one board; fit the other board over the protruding dowels and clamp the two together.

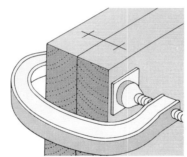
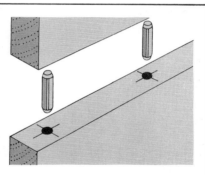

**1.** Clamp both boards together back to back when marking. Mark lines across and along each board—centers for dowels are where lines intersect.
**2.** Drill the dowel holes centrally and square, making sure they are deep enough. Chamfer the dowels at each end; groove them to let excess glue run out.

## Splined joint

These joints are more suitable for longer work and are easier to make accurately than doweled joints.

Cut the tongue (spline) from cross-grained plywood and select a plow-plane blade of exactly the same thickness, or groove the edges on a table saw.

Cut a groove along both prepared edges, running the plow fence along the face side. The combined depth of both grooves is just slightly greater than the width of the spline (1).

Glue and assemble the joint (2) and clamp the assembly together.

Make a final check for flatness, then wipe off any excess glue. Cut and trim for overall size only after the glue has set.

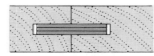
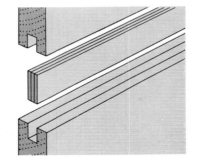
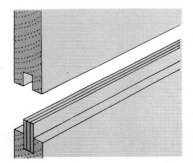

**1.** Cut the grooves to the exact width of the tongue. Make the combined depths of the grooves about 1/16 in. greater than the width of the spline.
**2.** Glue both edges and grooves. Fit the plywood spline into one board and set the other board on it. Clamp and check for flatness. Wipe off surplus glue.

Make grooves deeper than spline width

# Lengthening joints

## Choosing the correct joint

Lumber often has to be lengthened for big projects, such as garages, carports, or floor renovation. Smaller jobs, too, such as furniture repairing, occasionally require greater length than is available. What follows will give you a basis for selecting the proper joint, in terms of comparative strength and complexity of construction.

**Lapped joint:** The simplest of all the lengthening joints and suitable for use in lightweight structures. Cut the laps to half the thickness of the lumber; be sure that both shoulders butt exactly against the end of the joining pieces or the joint will be weakened.

Secure the joint with glue and screws. The screws should be staggered—this is in order to avoid splits along the grain.

**Splayed lap:** A variant of the half lap, with the lap cut in the thickness instead of the width. Can be used where the joint itself is supported by a joist or wall. Its chief use is to keep decorative, nonsupporting ceiling beams in line where center nailing has to be straight for fastening sheet materials such as wallboard.

Cut a splay along the grain to resist any tendency of the joint to pull apart. Make the length of the joint equal to the width of the lumber.

Drive a cut nail diagonally through the lower lap into the joist or supporting wall plate (lumber running along the top of the wall). Butt on the joining length and secure with another nail driven diagonally through from the top.

**Bolted joint:** Carriage bolts used with lumber connectors make strong face-to-face joints in beams and trusses.

Insert the connectors—metal washers with toothed edges—on the bolts between the joining faces. Tighten the nuts and the connectors will bite into the wood, increasing the shear strength of the joint. Use washers under the nuts.

**Using joining plates:** A sandwich construction using joining plates gives great strength to end-to-end joints. Cut the joining plates (sometimes called fish plates) four times longer than the width of the timber. They should be the same width as the lumber but only half its thickness.

Glue all surfaces, and stagger the screws or carriage bolts. Carriage bolts pass through the wood; screws should be just short of passing through.

**Scarf joint:** This is cut on a long slant and is used where great strength is required.

A scarf joint is usually just glued, but the angle-cut faces need to be cut and planed with great accuracy. Properly made, it is as strong as the lumber that it joins.

Ideally, the slant of the scarf should be eight to one or greater in order to achieve full wood strength. Screws need not be used for extra strength with modern resin glues. Clamp the joint while the glue is setting.

**V-spliced joint:** This is used mainly in furniture repairs or in applications where appearance is an important consideration.

Cut the V with a fine-tooth saw. Then cut and plane the joining piece to an exact fit. Glue the pieces, join, and clamp in position.

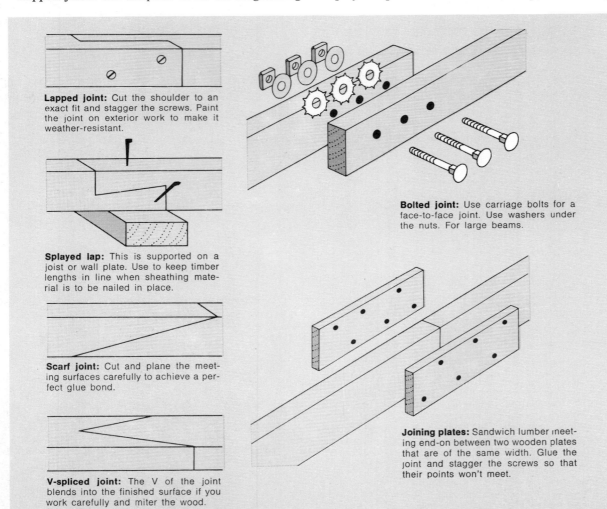

**Lapped joint:** Cut the shoulder to an exact fit and stagger the screws. Paint the joint on exterior work to make it weather-resistant.

**Splayed lap:** This is supported on a joist or wall plate. Use to keep timber lengths in line when sheathing material is to be nailed in place.

**Scarf joint:** Cut and plane the meeting surfaces carefully to achieve a perfect glue bond.

**V-spliced joint:** The V of the joint blends into the finished surface if you work carefully and miter the wood.

**Bolted joint:** Use carriage bolts for a face-to-face joint. Use washers under the nuts. For large beams.

**Joining plates:** Sandwich lumber meeting end-on between two wooden plates that are of the same width. Glue the joint and stagger the screws so that their points won't meet.

## Six ways to attach legs at corners

Three-way joints are essential for making tables and chairs and certain types of framing. Construction methods range from the use of glue and screws to doweling and tenoning.

A simple way of joining a leg to two rails is with a commercially produced chair and table corner brace that fits into slots in the rails (1). These braces come in a number of sizes. The joint is held together by a screw which is passed through the brace into the leg.

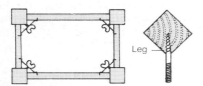

Frame fixed with chair corner braces

Some types of braces also provide holes for screws.

Mark the positions of the legs and rails on the underside of the chair or table top. Cut the rails to exact size. Position the braces at 45 degrees in the corners on the penciled outline and mark the location of the slots that will house the brace ends in the rails. Transfer these positions to the wood and cut the slots to fit.

Mark on the inner corner of each leg the place where the plate screw is to go and drill a hole deep enough for the wood screw to get a start.

Attach the rails to the table top with glue or small metal inside corner braces, then drive a hanger bolt into the pre-drilled hole in each leg. Insert the other end of the bolt in the corner plate and tighten the wing nut.

Dowels on corner joints (2) need to be staggered to prevent their meeting in the middle of the leg. Use at least three on each rail (if space permits) and space them evenly. The dowels should be one-third the thickness of the rails.

Glued and screwed corners are strong and can be made quickly. They can be arranged so that the leg is inside (3) or outside (4) the rails.

The strongest corner joint of all is the mitered mortise and tenon (5 and 6). Basically, the joint is just two rabbeted stub tenons meeting at right angles in the center of the leg.

Mark out and tenon the rails and mortise the inner

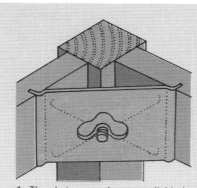

**1.** The chair corner brace, available in several sizes, holds corner together with a hanger bolt. The plate fits into slots in the rails.

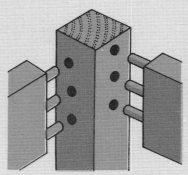

**2.** Dowels must be staggered to prevent their meeting in the middle of the leg. Space them as evenly as possible; use at least three to a rail.

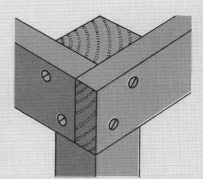

**3.** Glue and screw the rail to the legs for a quick and strong corner joint. Stagger the screws to prevent splits; countersink their heads.

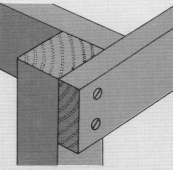

**4.** A similar joint can be made with the leg on the outside. Both joints rely solely on the strength of the glue and screws. Wood plugs can cover recessed screw heads.

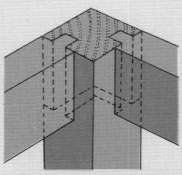

**5.** The haunched and mitered mortise and tenon is the strongest of the leg joints. Leave about ½ in. of waste at the top of the leg; trim it off when the joint is complete.

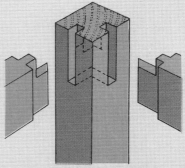

**6.** An exploded view of the joint, showing the miters on the ends of the tenons. Trim the miters so there is a small gap between them on assembly to allow for excess glue.

faces of the leg. Fit rails separately, then miter the tenon ends so there is a small gap between them when the joint is assembled.

Leave about ½ inch of waste at the top of the leg; trim it off when the joint is completed. This prevents splitting.

**Cabinet corner joints:** In cabinet construction, tongue and groove the panels into solid corner pieces. The tongue should be one-third the thickness of the panel.

Solid tongues can be cut at either surface of the panel, or the grooves can be cut into the panel ends and the tongues on the corner pieces. These joints are chiefly used with solid wood, not plywood.

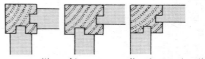

Joints vary position of tenon according to construction

# Basic structures

## Making a simple box

Learn to build this basic unit and you will be on your way to many more complex structures. The steps are easy to follow:

1. Fasten together the four sides of the box, each cut on the square.
2. Before attaching the back section (or bottom, as the case may be), nail two strips of wood diagonally across the front of the box to stiffen the structure and hold it square.
3. Nail or glue the back to the box; remove the strips. Should you wish to make your box into a bookcase, simply turn it on end and add shelves.
4. You can do this by attaching plastic tracks or molding to the sides and sliding the shelves into position. (Shelves may be nailed to molding.)
5. Tracks may also be produced by attaching two strips of molding on either side as shown.

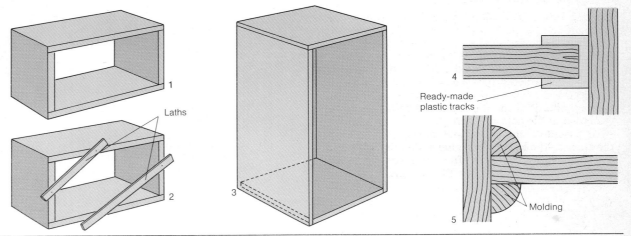

Laths

Ready-made plastic tracks

Molding

## Making a simple drawer

A drawer is simply a box, four sides and a bottom (1), but it can be constructed several ways. Drawing 2 shows the side pieces fitted into slots in the front, permitting nails to be driven from two directions (3) for extra stability.

By placing the bottom of the drawer in grooves cut in the side pieces (4), you provide a narrow bearing area between side and runner. The back slides into grooves in the sides; the bottom is grooved to the front. It is then possible to nail the bottom to the back and front from beneath.

In another variation (5), grooves are cut in the sides to act as tracks for runners, which are fastened to the walls of the basic unit (6).

In drawing 7, drawer fronts are slightly deeper than the drawers themselves, giving the unit, when they meet, a neat, finished look.

Instead of grooves, two strips of wood may be added, the slot between them acting as a track (8). Or single strips may be nailed to the sides as runners (9), which travel along grooves in the unit's side (10). Tracks may also be made by attaching twin strips to the unit's sides (11). Simplest of all: Ready-made plastic tracks (12).

A drawer may be suspended under a desk or table on L-shaped molding (13) or plastic tracks on wood strips (14), fastened in either case to the underside.

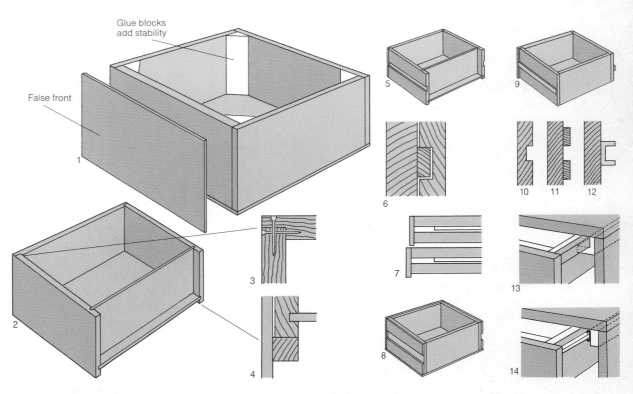

Glue blocks add stability

False front

## Rabbeted-front drawers

The rabbet and dado joint shown on the drawer at the right can be made easily on a table saw or radial arm saw with a dado head or by repeated passes over (or under) the saw blade, with the cutting depth adjusted to suit. The back of the drawer front, like the drawer back and sides, is dadoed to take the edge of the plywood bottom. If the drawer is to have side runners, the sides should be dadoed before assembly, as shown in the detail sketch.

To assemble the individual parts, you first join the sides to the back, using glue and nails. Next, slide the bottom panel in place after coating its edges, and the grooves into which they fit, with glue. Then coat the bottom dado and end rabbets of the drawer front with glue, along with the front edge of the bottom panel and the front ends of the sides, and fit the parts together. The angle nailing of the sides and front (as indicated) locks the assembly while the glue sets. If the stopped dadoes are made on a power saw, stop the saw cut well short of the dado end and finish to the stopping point with a chisel. Attach drawer hardware after glue has set.

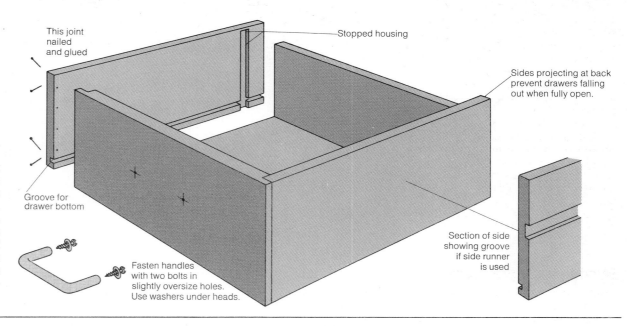

This joint nailed and glued

Stopped housing

Sides projecting at back prevent drawers falling out when fully open.

Groove for drawer bottom

Section of side showing groove if side runner is used

Fasten handles with two bolts in slightly oversize holes. Use washers under heads.

## Overlapping-front drawers

If the drawer front overlaps the sides, as in the unit at right, to conceal all framing behind it, the joint between the sides and front may be "dovetail dadoed" for added strength, as shown in the sketch at the lower right. The same type of joint (or a plain dado joint) may be used where the sides join the back. In either case the dado is stopped below the top, and, if it was cut on a power saw, finished with a chisel. The plywood bottom of the drawer is fitted in dadoes all around, as in the drawer above.

If you decide you want to make a dovetail dado, it can be easily cut by setting the saw for the desired depth of cut and adjusting the blade tilt to the dovetail angle. Use the same tilt in cutting the mating piece. If you have not previously made this type of joint on the saw, make a few trial joints in scrap wood to practice the technique. The plain dadoes to take the drawer bottom are made by simply setting the blade for the depth of cut and the fence for the correct distance from the edge. Reset the fence to shave the cuts to the groove width and remove intervening material with in-between passes.

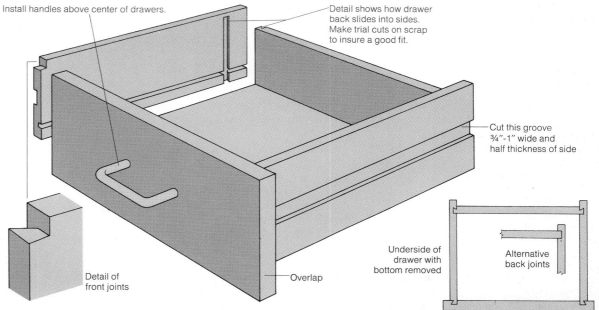

Install handles above center of drawers.

Detail shows how drawer back slides into sides. Make trial cuts on scrap to insure a good fit.

Cut this groove ¾"-1" wide and half thickness of side

Detail of front joints

Overlap

Underside of drawer with bottom removed

Alternative back joints

# Drawer construction

## Drawer guides

To assure that drawers move straight in and out without jamming at an angle, they can be equipped with tracklike guides. **Corner guides** fit around the lower outside corners of the drawer sides. The bottom of each guide serves as a supporting track, the raised portion as a curb to prevent turning. A "kicker" strip of wood is often mounted above the drawer to prevent the back from tipping upward (and the front downward) as the drawer nears full extension. **Side guides** consist of grooves in the outer surface of the drawer sides which fit stationary runners mounted in the frame of the furniture. As no additional support is necessary, the cross members between the drawers can be reduced in thickness or even eliminated, adding to overall drawer volume. **Center guides** consist of a grooved or twin rail unit

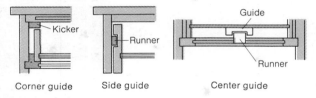

Corner guide    Side guide    Center guide

on the underside of the drawer with a stationary rail (attached to the framing) in the middle. This assures that the drawer moves straight in and out, while allowing clearance at the sides. The weight of the drawer may be supported by the lower edges of the sides riding on flat rails without the curb strips of corner guides.

All wood-to-wood guides operate more smoothly and easily if lubricated, either by waxing or applying a spray lubricant made for the purpose. In either case, the wood surface should first be given a coat of sealer and allowed to dry.

Manufactured drawer slides are available in many forms, usually comparable to the center guide and side guide, but with special advantages, including low-friction rollers. Full extension types with telescoping rails permit the drawer to be pulled out to its full length without disengaging or tipping. In planning for the use of ready-made slides, however, clearance at drawer sides or bottom must be allowed for the make and model of slide to be used. Typical clearances: Allow one inch for track between drawers with center slides and a half-inch clearance at sides for side slides.

## Hardware installation

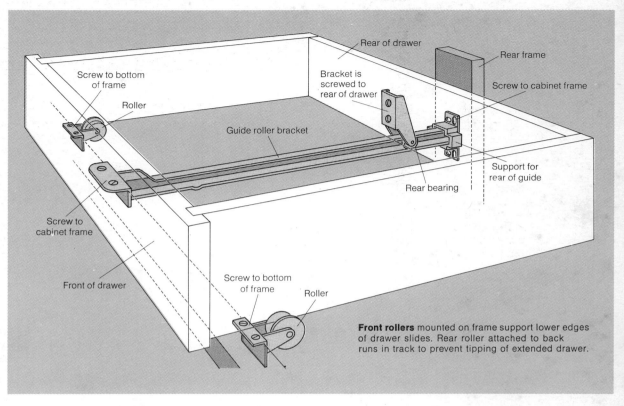

**Front rollers** mounted on frame support lower edges of drawer slides. Rear roller attached to back runs in track to prevent tipping of extended drawer.

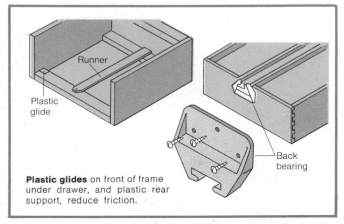

**Plastic glides** on front of frame under drawer, and plastic rear support, reduce friction.

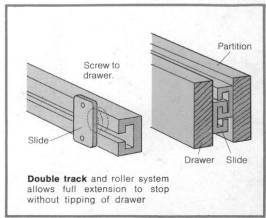

**Double track** and roller system allows full extension to stop without tipping of drawer